less than what you once were

a memoir

by

aaron brown

less than what you once were
Copyright © 2022 AARON BROWN
All Rights Reserved.
Published by Unsolicited Press.
Printed in the United States of America.
First Edition.

No part of this book may be used or reproduced in any manner whatsoever without written permission except in the case of brief quotations embodied in critical articles or reviews.

Attention schools and businesses: for discounted copies on large orders, please contact the publisher directly.

For information contact:
Unsolicited Press
Portland, Oregon
www.unsolicitedpress.com
orders@unsolicitedpress.com
619-354-8005

Cover Image: *Prolonged by a Hundred Shadows*, detail, 2019, painted twigs, paper, twine, 220 cm diameter © Anita Groener (photographer Louis Haugh)

Editor: Kristen Marckmann; Robin Ann Lee

ISBN: 978-1-956692-11-2

"…when I reach halfway memory lets go of my hand, and a fog rises and covers the faces and places, and I am left clawing about in the dark, lost, and I have to make up the obscured moments as I go along"

—Helon Habila

"We have a very precise image—an image at times shameless—of what we have lost, but we are ignorant of what may follow or replace it."

—Jorge Luis Borges

less than what you once were

I
N'Djamena
February 2, 2008

You begin with knowing air, dust-thick and fog-like from the fluorescents, the air that hovers between ceiling and floor littered with the little you have brought with you. Bags upturned, books and socks scattered. You walk out with the others into rooms you had been in a half-hour before. Before you had seen the figure outside the window, heard the sound of a single gunshot, your father yelling—out of fear? Out of pain?

You had found yourself alone, alone on the other end of the hall. Your family across the way crying, but you couldn't fit in the crevice where they hid. So you tried to stretch yourself across the wall, so as not to be seen through the windows. Tried to melt into the cream-colored wall, chameleon your skin so that it fit the safe borders.

But the figures outside, no longer one, gather at the kitchen door, and with a single shove of the crowbar, the kitchen gate clatters to the cracked patio.

You stumble with the others into the darkest bedroom. You recognize more than your parents—friends? Your father's coworkers. Their children. How much do you realize each of them are there? In this moment, you are only shadows scuttling along the silent cement floor. In the bedroom, one of them fiddles with keys at a door leading outside, his hands shaking so strongly he can't find the right one, can't get you out.

You hear the figures come into the kitchen, then the hall where you just were. You watch your father walk out to meet them. You hear them speak to him, muffled. You do not know what they are doing but you hear the scuff of their sandals. You find out later they were speaking to your dad and hitting him. *Show us where the money is.* Hit. *Car keys.* Hit. *Laptop.* Hit.

You come face to face with one of them. A boy, just like you. He is wearing a zipped-up AC Milan jacket. Nervous, because he did not expect to find you, hiding with the others in the back bedroom. He stands taller, wets the dry roof of his mouth. Asks for all you have. One man gives him his advance of three months' salary, just received in a paper envelope. Another, a cell phone. The boy takes these. He looks to his right, opens a desk drawer, stares at what's inside. Shuts it without taking anything.

He is gone. They are gone. One by one, vehicles out in the yard light up, back out until the yard is empty. The rooms, empty. Only the air is full. Latent, static.

You walk out with the others, adrenaline anointing your forehead, pouring down your shoulders like holy water. The house has been overturned—in minutes made to look like harmattan-swept fields. Belongings scattered, a fresh layer of dust caking the soles of your feet. Above, the lightbulbs buzz. A moth taps the glass, desiring to be let in.

You go to your small backpack where you left it. Its contents are missing except for the toothbrush, change of clothes. You are grateful for the breath you take, the heart whose rhythm's slowed.

We'll go to the landlord's, someone speaks. The voice so loud it seems gun-fresh, like the looters' warning shot.

Alley cats, you and the others peer out the street gate. Empty. You scurry across the way. The landlord's son comes out to meet you. Knew something was wrong when the shot sounded from this street and not the other streets, the ones still covered with today's bullet casings. You file in with the others. Into the yard—mango tree, a radio with a wire stretching up to the tip of the brick wall, glass shard guarded. A woman's voice on the radio, French. Sounding off the world's news. A football transfer. A monsoon in India. Another war a thousand kilometers away.

With your mother, you are invited into the room of the landlord's wife. Plush carpets. Low couches covered in pink polyester with gold trim. She gives you biscuits. Guava juice. You thank her. She turns on the television. A soap opera. Tomorrow you will watch the same screen as Gaddafi shakes his fist, says he has negotiated a ceasefire between your president and the rebels. You will see this news as a helicopter is hit by a rocket-propelled grenade above you. You will hear the clips emptied again in the streets. You will feel the walls shudder like ribcages.

You have left the room of your companions. Left them to steep in their own sorrowful talk. To see their room fade and crumble around. Crumble to rubble, but still they remain talking. You walked out a body, became a shadow. You became a shadow that tries to get back. Tries to find its flesh again.

You are driving somewhere in Maryland, the highway packed with four-lanes of 70 mph drivers, when you receive the call. Your wife picks up, and you can tell from the way she responds that something is wrong. It's your father, and you can decipher that you need to call him back. *Some difficult news.* When you arrive at your destination—where your wife's aunt and uncle live—you go into a room and shut the door. You hold the phone up, feel the dead weight of your heart sink into the void of gut, knowing that some terrible thing has happened to someone you love. The familiar feeling. The same feeling that doesn't lessen or worsen but only remains the same rattling pain, down to your bone core.

"It's Madri," your father says when you finally press to return his call.

It's as if you knew. Your father starts to talk. Madri was riding his motorcycle to work in the morning. There was an accident—the circumstances unclear. They took him to the hospital, medicated him, released him. After several hours at home, the hospital calls back to say they need to see him again immediately. When next he is admitted, he does not exit the hospital again alive.

You start to gasp, the realization shifting to the slow-drip knowing that a close friend, a brother to you and your brother, a son to your father, is gone and is not coming back. No more tea underneath the hajlij tree. No more of that sheepish grin, the leaning back behind his office desk, pausing work always for conversation. No more spotting him a long way off, coming down the road, slender and confident. The man every person in the neighborhood felt blessed to be greeted by, to know as a friend, to be treated as family. You feel again the distance of ocean. You know the wailing and the weeping and the ripping of clothing that is happening back home. You know the wind is kicking up at dusk now, and the cows are coming into town, and the maghrib muezzin is sounding the call to prayer as rows of men ablute themselves, pray along the streets, then meander to Madri's home. You know the streets are swelling with those who've come to mourn a brother, too.

But you are not there to join them.

The rooms of your house are empty. The windows let in the wind like taking in breath. You turn and find in one room a skeleton, a shape of what you once were, and you realize spirit has been separated from flesh. You hover strangely above the ground, floating around as if in one moment the wind could dissipate you into a thousand scattered particles. Return to the dust that made you. Return to the air that formed you. This is, after all, the cleaving knife that separated your soul and body down to the core. Rent apart, there is no return to your previous state. When the air and earth were one. When body and soul spoke to one another.

 Spirit of a ghost.

A hush spreads throughout the men gathered on the mat as the faki raises his two hands in prayer, lacing his supplication with the names of God and the delicate words of the Quran. There is time as he prays for the falcon overhead to cross from one horizon to the other. When he lowers his hands, Madri's brother Djamile leans forward to whisper his new baby girl's name into the faki's ear. Like wakened wind through rainy season gesh, the name passes from man to man, until it reaches you, lounging beside Madri, his lips parted in the proud smile of an uncle.

You lean forward, inquire what his new niece's name is. "Sakina," he replies. *Peace,* you know it means. *Serenity.* How soon your friend will find his own peace in the soot-cloud future.

"Now let me ask you the name of your girlfriend." Madri's eyes light with humor.

"Melinda," you tell him.

"Me-lin-da," he tastes the word. "Your sadikti must be beautiful."

You have pictures of that final flight from Ati when you and your parents were to return to America, leaving behind the dust-covered town you'd name as home for almost a decade. There is Madri standing quietly. Imam, too, and Issa, Mahamat Tahir, Al Goni, and Abdelmadjid. The Sahel wind whips around their clothes, waves forever solidified in a photo. Each has a somber look on his face. You know it was mirrored in your own.

Like many erasures, those who have passed on disappear from the picture. Madri dying. Al Goni traveling across countries for an education. You intend to visit again soon, to wrestle with the pain of their different departures. But for those who have remained behind, what will you say to them? How can you express your grief for a lost friend? How can you express your regret for the poor efforts you have taken to reach out across the oceanic divide in the years since? How will you find the words?

You have returned. Footprints in a thick layer of dust. Suitcases with airplane tags in a pile in the corner. You lie in your bed and listen to the street sounds with the lights outside shining through the shutters, webbing shadows over your face. Crickets tick away the hours from underneath the bed. Outside, two men are talking, but you only hear sounds and not words. A motorcycle takes minutes to whir by and minutes more to fade into the night.

A bang from the street, and you are awake, heart beating faster. But you can no longer think of emptied gun clips. You must sleep even when a car backfires.

You ride the escalator down to the departure lounge for what the airline has deemed second-class citizens—an unremodeled sea of plastic chairs packed with men and women dressed in everything from grand boubous to abayas, jellabiyas to pin-striped suits. Glass walls frame the packed area with signs reading *Bamako, Khartoum, Doula, N'Djamena*. It's the last sign you find yourself under as the boarding announcement is made.

The people swarming the counter look like an assortment of the people you've known since childhood—the wealthy N'Djamena boy with Nikes and a button-up shirt, playing some video game in one hand while slurping a milkshake in the other; two conservatively dressed teenagers who must be brothers, their captaniyes immaculately pressed clean so that yards of fabric lie so straight their polyester fibers catch the recessed lights above like a mirror; even a white woman, some medical or aid worker—the kind of person you would encounter at night, at a bar or standing outside the house gate, always another white person asking questions—Why have you come? What can you offer?—and you hardly haveing answers.

When you board and find your seat by the window, a whole troop of teenagers come down the aisle and nudge each other as they unsling their bags before taking a seat to cycle through all the movies available on their seat console.

"Adoudou, make sure my bag fits up there," one boy urges his friend who has an aisle seat, handing him a backpack to be placed in the overhead compartment. Adoudou finds a crack between the luggage, proceeds to cram the bag in there. "Be gentle!"

It is now that a five-year absence collapses in the space of a second. You find yourself surrounded again by the cadence of Arabic—and not the Arabic of Jordan or Cairo or Saudi, the Arabic everyone assumes you'll understand but strain to—no, the Arabic of home, the slang-filled hybrid of street-French and Arabic and other words coming from the corners of the Sahel.

You listen to the others talk about the airline food, the weather, the stuffy seats. You listen to an old man in a grand boubou complain about his sore leg. "I went to Abu Dhabi for a consultation," he tells a businessman next to him. "But they said it cannot be operated on. I am too old," he chuckles to himself.

You watch as an elderly mother, ailing yet still dressed in her finest, is uprooted along with her adult children by a Nigerian man holding up his ticket and pointing at the seat number. The woman and her children shuffle to the row of seats behind and sit down with a collective huff.

When the plane lands in Kano for a brief stop-off and the humid Sahel summer air seeps into the cabin, you feel the realness of return to the African continent: the latent scent at midnight in the weeks leading up to rainy season, when the bugs start to slowly increase in numbers, and the air suspends itself in a wet blanket of humidity. Fresh life waiting—if only the clouds would open up and release their stores. Sometimes, you trick yourself into catching the same smells in America, in April when that perfect mix of dust and wet get mixed together in the air. But even then you know it to be a poor substitute.

From Kano to N'Djamena, Chad's capital, it is a short flight of an hour and a half. You stretch over your father's seat to get a glimpse through the window of any signs of life. You pass over a city, which must have been one of the border towns Nigeria shares with Cameroon. From the distance of thousands of feet, you see some kind of brushfire. You remember the time when you were seventeen driving across the same plains in Cameroon, lines of fire stretching out parallel to the road. As if the apocalypse had come to slowly constrict life with flame. An omen only months before your world started to end, before the shot rang out on the street and you thought your father dead, before the months you spent away from this place, a taste of the years that followed.

When you see her again, you don't expect for her to crumple in your arms and weep and say her dead son's name over and over again—*Madri, Madri*.

You are the first of your family to enter the yard, the first afternoon you are back in town, back on the continent. One of her sons has seen you far off, nodding silently, reverently—as if knowing the mourning that would come—before he disappears through the doorway to warn her. And when you come inside—the immaculate concession yard swept to a speck, everything in its proper place—you see her thin frame, covered by a calico dress, and her face dipping into sorrow. You try a smile, but realize within a second that this is not the time. You are entering a house of mourning—the thick of it still present a year after his passing.

Your parents and your brother filter in behind you, and for the next hour, your family weeps alongside the woman who is your self-proclaimed grandmother. Your brother, Bentley, placing his hands over his eyes, tears streaming, and you—staring out at the tree waving above you. Hearing the muffled sobs. Young Mahamat Tahir, his pre-teen body only just beginning to lengthen, sits next to your brother. *Don't cry. Don't cry.*

When the tears run out, and the dry wind speaks across the sand-swept yard, your grandmother brings out a photo album, and she asks a daughter to bring biscuits and tea. Then, underneath the thatch lugdabe, she flips each page, one and then the other. All that we had not been present to see. Madri and his engagement. Madri and his new wife. Madri and the infant son. The son who was barely a week old when his father passed. You hear your grandmother speak of the house he was building on the outskirts of town—a house with red brick, cement, plaster, and a tin roof—a place the whole family would be proud of. You hear her talk about his widow and how she couldn't get along with the family, and finally, exhausted, took the child away from them all as she returned to her parents' town in Oum Hadjer.

There is only one photo of the new family. Of a boy with the amber skin of his father. The slender face. Though the print is fuzzy, you catch sight of the same gleaming eyes. The eyes that light like lantern flame at a joke, always at the edge of mirth. Surrounding the child, the parents cradle the boy in their arms together. Lips spread wide, they smile for the new life they hold—and in the smile, there is no hint of the coming suffering, the coming loss. Only hindsight lurks with full weight beyond the frame. A picture freezing a moment when this family is at peace, when everything is as it should be before it is ripped apart.

The picture book is soon closed. The tea glasses emptied. The dusk wind picks up beside you as the words between your families linger in the spaces between the wind.

When finally your family gets up to leave—assuring your grandmother that you will be back tomorrow and every day for the two-week-long visit—there is an intermixed lightness and heaviness you feel, weighing then lifting your shoulders and weighing them again. The feeling that the earth is not so far from the sky as you previously thought. The feeling that the land of the living and the land of the dead often converge into one.

Over lunch that day you discuss what happened to Madri. A year has passed since his death but you are no closer to unearthing the truth than when you started. Your father's friend, Abakar, the loyal mechanic turned entrepreneur who now runs half the town, speaks in his slow cadence, measuring the words of his speculations. *He was so sad when you left.* The worry, the stress of managing a hospital, had all begun to wear on Madri. He had a new wife after all, a woman his family didn't seem to accept. So his heart hurt to the point of rupture, or did it? So he found solace in pills he grabbed off the hospital shelves, or did he? So he hit the mud wall on his motorcycle head on, snapping his ribs and femurs and skull, or did he?

What becomes clear, from this conversation and others, is that Madri did in fact slow his motorcycle to a stop. There was no other bike or car. He was alone on the road, a wide expanse of dirt and sand so even if he had fallen, it would have been difficult to fracture bone. There was the barb-wired prison in the distance and some guards or inmates or both sitting on the mat together sipping tea. But they were just far enough away to barely see what happened. There was a woman, too, walking from the market or a friend's house, her lafiye blanketed in the crimson shades of sand crystals. She saw Madri, too. Saw him stop the bike, get off. Collapse onto the sand.

How then did he make it to the hospital, get released then called back? Shot through with so much pain medication did they cause his heart to stop, his brain to bleed? Or was there something else?

You eat lunch, listen to your father's friend talk. *The street around their house was covered in mats and the mourners that sat on them.* You are left to imagine what that must have looked like.

You had returned to Chad, returned for two weeks, and come back. You had not seen everyone, could not see everyone. And now, somewhere inside of you, memory's backbone tries to recreate those who were not there. Next, will you try and bring back the dead?

In the dream, you walk out of your house in Ati—the old house you lived in for so long. The yard shaded by the sighing hajlij tree. In the distance, the electric millet mill pounds grain to dust with a regularity that is soothing. Years later, you will think how similar the mill sounds to a Kalashnikov.

But now, here in the dream, to remove this familiar sound is to remove a bit of home. As if the sun were to stop lighting the world and the sand were to cease sliding sideways underfoot.

Someone—your father or mother—has told you to come outside. That a friend is waiting. They say it with hushed excitement, knowing the joy you will feel when seeing a friend long lost to distance. You walk out to the circle of chairs, just as there always had been: neighbors and coworkers all gathered around your father—laughing as they sip mint tea and grab handfuls of peanuts.

And on the steps to the side guestroom, you notice a small body: a boy with head bowed so that you cannot see his face. His thin frame dressed in clothes that must have been plucked fresh from the tailor's shop. As you approach, he raises his head, and it is then you recognize Al Goni, one of your dearest friends, with whom you have spent hours playing basketball, talking about everything from English to rebel movements to Ramadan fasting. He smiles and you feel as glad as you feel surprised, thinking that he isn't supposed to be here. That he is far away in Burkina. And how did he rush back so quickly just to see you before you returned to America? And what would you do together in the remaining hours? Would you go out past the forest to the riverbed? Would you walk among the deep trenches in the earth where brickmakers dig out the soil to make their giant kilns? Would you throw rocks at the remains of an old war plane—French or Libyan—that baked in the sun for half a century, so long ago that the story of its crashing has been lost?

You are spared the choice. You wake and with waking, you realize that you aren't with him, that you don't have one more day to spend walking around Ati. That you are alone, in an apartment in Maryland.

The wind picks up before you have the time to see the sky has grown thick with cloud, the trees in the distance sway with wind, and the sand is pockmarked with silent droplets, testing the ground as if to ask if torrents should rain down, overflowing the banks of heaven. What begins as a gentle sweep of sand becomes violent—ripping branches off from trees, causing the hajlij fruit to shatter on the ground, bringing the thunder to your ears with the speed of tempestuous gusts. Then the rain showers down, rising within seconds to a roar—it fills all sound and exceeds, drumming on the tin as if a thousand synchronous drumsticks. It thunders for an hour, but the time seems so short. The rain halts, the clouds recede, and just like that the ground is saturated, water trickling down the alleyway by the house with the blue gate.

They come through the gate, telling the family hosting you, protecting you, that the rebels have spread the word in the neighborhood to get out. They say the rebels are about to begin a new offensive, establish a new front vying for the president's palace over on the Chari River, fifteen minutes away.

Your father and the others deliberate for a few minutes. *Is this our chance?* And then your father tells you to get your backpack and then all ten of you are piling into the truck and the engine is running and the gate pulls back and you are driving out onto the paved road and there are women holding their children's hands while balancing their belongings on top of their heads and there are men with the radio antennas fully extended listening to the latest news and waiting on benches for the rebels to drive by, and as the truck bounces forward on a road that has few other cars your heart pounds harder than the submachine gun that emptied itself out on the street the day before when you almost left the house then and walked straight into a hotbed of bullets.

When the truck pulls out onto Avenue Nimarie, you are struck by how silent the street is. At first, no cars, no trucks, no barricades. People hang halfway out of open doors watching warily. And then you see abandoned Peugeots and mopeds beginning to pepper the street and the fallen branches of the giant neem trees planted by the French. You pass the high school where you once played basketball with your brother and the students there until you slipped and lodged a piece of gravel in your knee, then walked all the way home with blood trickling down your leg. You turn onto the streets of dignitaries and the UN—the stuffy streets, the ones where the only signs of life usually are the guards hanging around on blue-stringed chairs, listening to Boys 2 Men or Magic System.

But today, these streets have no living bodies. You pass by a car in flames but you do not look inside of it. Your truck, all of you in this sweaty truck, stops at the gate of the French lycee you had heard about for years but never bothered going to. A French soldier comes out, takes your passports. You hear the mother of your friend cry out, and you look down the road and see a train of tanks and armored personnel carriers barreling toward you. For a second, you think it is some gun-happy enemy, but you can tell somehow, perhaps through the sand-colored paint or the lack of urgency with which they drive, that they are neutral. Even then, you hope the soldier will let you in before the convoy comes and you find out whether your conclusions are true or false.

And the soldier does let you in and you all get out of the truck, folding out of the three seat rows then unfolding onto the tarmac of a tree-lined parking lot oddly untouched by the war outside its gates. The French soldiers talk to your father and a colleague on the patio, the light gleaming gold across the tiles that have been scraped clean by the sandals of boys and girls for decades. Outside, you hear a side gate rattle. And one of the personnel carriers you saw earlier rolls in and your father says you are all getting in and the hatch doors open and it is hot—no windows—and you think for a second how thrilling it is to be carried in a tank version of a minivan until it lurches out onto the street and speeds right then left then forward then left then right. And you know the way it's going, past the smoldering cars, around the roundabout with the giant sugarcane statue and probably some abandoned goat tied to a bench in its little garden park. You know it is driving past the military barracks of the Chadian army—abandoned or heavily guarded?—you can't see. You only know that it is driving beyond all this, and then down streets you have never gone before, somewhere where the French military base slumbers outside of town. Slumbers in the shadows of colonial buildings, the paint fading, walls ship-shoddily patched. The vehicle slows, finally, and the top hatch opens, and you see trees above, the kind of ancient trees with roots that run deep into the nearby Chari river.

    Clutching your bag to your chest, you remember then the hoodie you left back in the truck, on the backseat where you had hunched close to the window, looking out, or between the seats as you climbed out a side door. You will not see that hoodie for months just as you will not see the rest of your belongings, your home, your friends—months you spend wandering around the streets of Paris, shivering with longing for what you had. The days you spend walking after the sun sets along Montparnasse or out along the Seine, trying to find your way back. And you do find your way back, and for some reason, you still have that hoodie, now hung up on a back rung in your utility room. So often when you wear it, going out for a jog in winter, the chilled Midwest air biting through, you forget that you forgot it, left it in a car in a school in a city ripped apart by war. A city you returned to months later, and then again, years later, to find that it was becoming less of itself, never the same again.

You wait with hordes of others in something resembling a cage clinging to the airplane hangar wall. Bleary-eyed, those around you clutch at the single bag they have with them—nothing else. In each facial line, you wonder what trauma lurks, wonder if the same veiled weight lurks within your own expression. Here is a single man, a journalist? Shirt half unbuttoned though he doesn't realize it. Tall, he stands above the rest looking through his rimless glasses to the tarmac in the dark, the C-130 that is being made ready for the passengers. Beyond the fluorescent bulb illuminating other expatriates (are you one?) or nationals with dual passports (or is this you?), you watch the flight crew—a darkly uniformed group of French military, who make the final checks of the airplane.

The gate to the cage is thrust aside, and the French soldiers motion for the group to move forward in a line. For a moment, you forget your fear of flying: you have lived through greater fears in the past two days—that a bullet or a grenade or the machete of a looter might sever sinew from bone, might shred ventricle or larynx and leave you struggling for air.

Here in the dark of night, leaving the way the looters who scaled your walls came—in light's utter absence—you cling close to your parents, not wanting to see them go. You fear you'll be pulled back and told the plane is full, that you must wait to get out, hours later. Your parents barreling up into the night, leaving you behind.

But everything is fine. You walk up the tail door of the C-130 into the belly of the aluminum beast, and inside, metal frame of the aircraft rimming above like ribs, you find a place on the canvas mesh seats. You strap yourself in, like an airman waiting to lift off on a mission, and you place your backpack in your lap, try to fall asleep, but your heart still pounds from the last two days, though it is an easier pound, one not of fear but of certainty emerging from adrenaline.

The others—families, journalists, dignitaries—all find their place on the red mesh. Soldiers come and check their fastenings one by one. The propellers at this point are deafening. The lights, like penlights, illuminate the shadows of the others as if you were travelling in the hull of a ship. The engines grow louder, the plane revs forward, and the wings tilt back, the aircraft bullets upward as quickly as it can out of range of fire.

You know you are being taken to another French military base in Gabon, but after that, when your passport is stamped and scanned and you are labeled a displaced person, where will you go? You think in this moment of your friends you have left behind in N'Djamena, how they will continue to sip tea under the neem trees, only now their streets are littered with bullet casings. Or you think of your hometown, Ati—how little it was touched apart from the rebel trucks speeding through. You imagine Atayib or Al Goni waking up each morning and knowing their country is in flames, yet looking out on the sandy streets and not seeing it. They will know only the crushing weight of what is coming, and what has already happened elsewhere. That there is no destination a truck can take them to anymore within these borders. That there is only the large expanse of sky above their heads that won't fill up with rain clouds for another five months, that won't bring life again to the dead land until the seasons change. You will imagine them looking up into the sky and wondering all this, and somewhere in their thoughts wondering where and why Haroun has fled again.

II
N'Djamena
April 26, 1999

You are eight years old, and it is in the middle of the night, the airplane door thrust open to air laden with water, dust, and life—some petrichoric smell you will grow used to, long for in the years to come. You walk down the metal stairs, struggling with a suitcase half your size. Yellow block letters blink across the awning of the nearby terminal A É R O P O R T H A S S A N D J A M O U S S.

At the base of the stairs, there is a rickety bus waiting, half-lit and sweltering in the midnight heat. The bus will fill with almost the entire passenger load, then circle around across the tarmac to the terminal barely a hundred yards away. You huddle next to your parents, your brother, even though it's warm, your heart pounding. The adventure, the reason your parents packed up and sold everything you had from the stucco house in Florida, the reason your life for the past year has been an itinerant one—from the training your father received in Virginia, then the further schooling, seminary, in Texas. Everything has led up to this stepping off of an Air France plane, painted French flag on the tail illuminated by a single spotlight. And the steps up into the terminal, the doors flanked by Chadian soldiers in camo and berets.

Three passport lines for foreigners and one for citizens, your father and mother lead you to a line, walk up to the attendant in the booth, fumble a mix of English and book-learned French, then find a way past the booth and on to baggage claim. In the future, you will blaze through this line with your Arabic, and the attendants will laugh at the white family who speaks it.

At baggage claim, the belt creaks along slower than the pace of a donkey at midday (you will find out later what that is like). Men in blue uniforms, some of them with skin the color of night and others with skin as light as the sands, push through with carts, vying for your father's attention. You will learn later of each skin's richness—whether a friend is Arab or Bilala, Sara or Hajari: each with the features that tell you where they are from, what history they are a part of, what identity they claim with grace and pride. You will wish your white skin could read with the same kind of history, and not one always pointing in the direction of privilege, of oppression.

Two men help your family with the bags, piling onto their carts each bag as it comes—1, 2, 3, 4—until you have upwards of ten bags, your parents overpacking your life while at the same time trying to get a start with your father's medical work: pill boxes packed in Ziploc bags, stethoscope padded by t-shirts, your basketballs and stuffed animals crammed in between.

You walk your bags, an entire caravan now, through the declaration tables. Official-looking men unzip the duffels, look to your father, remark vigorously about some associated cost, repeat a number—*dix milles* CFA—before finally giving up and waving this train of bags and family through. Years later, when you describe these first memories, your Ati friends will laugh at the airport officials, notoriously corrupt, and their X-ray machine used to sift through everything brought into the country. A national joke. The same machine that idles when the power goes out. The same machine that breaks for nine months out of the year, and lies unattended—a yellow box only convenient for placing Coke cans and declaration slips on top of.

You pass through the gate into the open box-like foyer of the airport. The space extends far above you, the walls painted in the style of cave paintings—mirrored after those found in the Tibesti mountains to the north—and the paintings surrounded by a trim the color of earth. Underneath the artwork, women in teal lafiyes, gold-embroidered, wait beside husbands eagerly jangling keys, searching the arriving passengers for familiar faces.

But the colleague who had promised your father that he'd be there is nowhere to be seen, and through the windows out toward the parking lot, you see only slumbering cars, the silhouettes of giant trees, and night. A nearby man sees you, some wandering American family, sleepless and looking around a terminal in a country that is their new home. He speaks, his accent American, and he knows your father's friend, knows where they live and volunteers to drive you there.

The clock on his dashboard blinks *3:06 a.m.* as the truck shudders out of the airport grounds, down streets lined with cement walls topped with barbed wire. But in the headlight-lit night, you see just the first flashes of the place you will come to love: the checkered street curbs, the pavement where asphalt disappears into dust and sand on the edges, the drains running along each street (you will jump out a car the next day and land in knee-deep open sewer to the laughter of everyone around you).

As the truck pulls first to the friend's house, you think you spot small creatures—you had done your research after all—a hedgehog battling with a snake, a small fennec fox traipsing down a dirt road. You excitedly turn from the window and point, telling the others what you see, and they strain their eyes in the dark too and chuckle about a tiger-striped bag and thin aqua bottle and yellow shoe, stuck in the sand. You are so tired you do not realize you are seeing visions.

The herd of camels encircles the village. The beasts shift silently on their feet with the moon giving birth to their shadows—these spirits watching over you, among you. You are sleeping across a mat laid out on the sand-grass. One man mumbles something, another ventures out into the dark to relieve himself. Still, others muse about the world in hushed tones.

Finally, the dawn draws everyone from sleep. You feel the moisture of dew in every fiber of your clothes, in every dead blade of the grass mat. You lie still as the men perform ablutions, washing with vigor their feet and arms and hands. They join together to pray towards the sunrise, to the bustling Mecca in another world. One of the nomads walks to the nearest camel and empties her of milk, bringing the now full bowl. You take a long sip and pass it on.

In the cool N'Djamena mornings, the sun finding its way down in between the papaya leaves, you find your first hedgehogs sniveling the ground with their barely perceptible grunts and ever-twitching noses. You find that if you spend hours petting their spikes, they grow used to you, their spikes laying down like soft fur as they unravel, expose their belly, and look at you with something mirroring caution and love. Your father decides to build a hedgehog home for you and your brother—a two-storied, screened-in cage with ample room for each hedgehog you'd catch. You watch them for hours, or hold them in your hand, walk up the steps to the roof of your house, Moussa teaching you your first words of Arabic—*aboungounfout yakhoul ful.* You laugh at the way the words catch on your tongue, and you laugh later at the way the words form into a sentence you hardly have need for—*The hedgehog eats peanuts.*

    You let the hedgehogs climb up and down the steps, you hold them as you watch the city traffic bustle blocks down on the paved road.

    Your hedgehogs grow, but they cannot be contained. It is then that Moussa shares with you the myths. *If you find a hedgehog in a street, place a bucket over it then remove it—the hedgehog will have disappeared.* You begin to find the cage empty in the mornings, no sign of escape, but somehow they had found a way out. Othertimes, you find the extent to which they had tried to leave, a hedgehog clinging to the chicken wire, almost free but bloodied and dead from an alley cat's clawmarks. So you and your brother decide to begin naming them the names of *Great Escape* characters, that old 1963 movie you had just watched for the first time about trapped POWs attempting escape from a Nazi concentration camp. There was Hilts, the suave, curious hedgehog, whose spikes couldn't be tamed. There was Ives, the baby, who curled up into the size of a quarter when you first got him. He started to grow too, and he was your favorite, the way his spikes never extended, and even then, had not grown into a sharp hardness, still almost like fur. Wanting to play with him one morning, you come to the cage and find him drowned in the water bowl.

It is then that you and your brother stop catching the aboungounfout, but would let them run free in the bushes. It is then you realize that some animals are not meant to be caught.

When after the first year you and your family move to the small dust-covered town you would call home, Ati, when your capital of millions becomes a town of ten thousand, you find a hedgehog on the first night there, too, out on the street at twilight, you sitting there and it coming on by. You clutch the familiar heart-beating orb in your hands once again, work on softening its spikes with steady caresses. Moussa sitting next to you, having moved his family out with yours to continue his employment, to continue his uncle-like role over you, to shepherd this hedgehog imagination within you.

And when a man comes by, the half-drunk man who works on the construction crew that had come to fix up your family's house, when he comes by and asks what it is you are holding, you lift up the hedgehog and smile. But then he does something you do not expect. He sneers at you, grabs the hedgehog from your hands, chucks it twenty yards into the twilight air. You watch the spiky orb rise up into the dusk air, rise and curl, and fall until it thuds into the ground in a dust cloud.

You find the hedgehog lying down the street, its body seizing and silent and the tears streaming down your face. You bring it into your flashlight lit room and set the animal down in a newly made box. You stay up that night, trying to feed it the peanuts you were told that it liked. You speak to it, too, hoping your words would console the animal while your own body shakes. You cannot explain why your body shakes.

When you bury the hedgehog in the morning, you are sure you'll never love a creature that much again. In the months that follow, you watch a seed from the overhanging hajlij tree fall and sprout in the place where you buried your friend. How quickly do you forget—as the small sprout grows branches you'll try and pluck but can never get rid of—that this is the place where you buried your last hedgehog?

You had a dog once. Your family had picked it out from a litter of mutts in a house by the giant buda, an open trash heap extending for miles before being submerged by rainy season water, tricking newcomers that it was some pretty lake until the dry season evaporated the water, leaving behind the stinking flesh of trash-filled ground.

You brought the dog home, sat out on the tiled patio, the patio where Moussa's radio shows were always going. And you first pet the small pup curled up in your woven legs. You remembered your family's first dog, buried in the backyard of the house where you spent your first years in Florida, a mystery of death your four-year-old brain could not quite answer. But here, here was the first ball of fur you were giving yourself over to—the dog you'd play with in light, the pup that howled its first night in your house, mourning the loss of its mother and siblings.

Your friends, your neighbors, your father's employees all thought it odd, the kind of love you could show a dog in a world where the edicts of folk Islam dictated that dogs are the vessels of shaytan, the dirt of the earth, hardly fit for scraps and only good for circling farms to protect them, nothing more. When you, the white boy, cradled the shaytan in your arms, no wonder Moussa and your neighbors laughed nervously, these the first days you realized your difference. Embarrassingly, you one time put a tagiye, a religious cap on its head and thought it funny, until the men around you shook their heads, hushed your laughter, told you to remove the hat quickly.

Your dog only wanted to protect you when it growled when others came near. The more she began to growl, the more she huddled close to your growing legs, trying to bar friends away from you, the more your parents looked at each other. The more they whispered plans you could not hear.

Finally, when your parents readied you and your brother for the cross-country move, from the capital with its high walls, grass trees, and bullet holes still unfilled after years of civil war, to Ati—you were told your dog could not come with you. It was one thing for cityfolk to deal with a dog, another for the people of a small town to somehow come to terms with a protective pup confined to a small yard.

You were still so young then, you didn't quite understand the full meaning of what was happening when your parents loaded up the car, you and your brother and your dog in the back. You stroked her back as your father pulled the truck through the city streets—the sea of lean-tos set up for market, the yellowed taxis shuddering forward around you. The long turn on the city outskirts where large market trucks slumbered under trees, their hoods open, rusted innards exposed for some mechanic to come and toy around with their rattling parts.

When the city had long faded, and only the occasional village cropped up, your car slowed along the road you would later take to your new home. The town between farms and the dry river, but still so far away, still so clouded in the unknown. Here along this deserted stretch of road, your father got out, some kind of sad understanding on his face, before he opened the two rear doors for you to climb down. "There's a small village nearby. Maybe she will be taken care of by them." Maybe she would be tossed some scrap of food, a half-chewed bone by a farmer's boy. When your father said these things, you wanted to believe them.

You played with her in the sand by the side of the road. And then your father told you to get back in the truck. As you pulled away, your brother wept silently beside you. You did not fully understand. You looked out the back window caked in dust, the sand kicked up behind the wheels. You could see her small brown frame staring at your wake, first confused, then running after you, her long legs fully extended to a sprint that could not match the speed of the truck. She is still running after you.

When you are barely ten, you and your brother take the rubber-wrapped slingshots, purchased from a merchant visiting your yard, out to the forest by the Batha River. The wild nabakh, dom, and spike-leafed trees clump together in thickets, ground cracked like skin, before the rows and rows of neems planted long ago by the French colonizers or some Chadian initiative to fight the growing desert. The goat herds graze underneath their leaves.

Like hunters, you creep forward through the forest sometimes at a crouch, sometimes at full stride, Atayib leading the way. Moussa towers behind, a man smiling like the boys around him. You find pebbles at your feet, hear the flitter of birds. You shoot and watch the small flocks fly out into the sky, circle back and land again, not too far away, not too afraid of your aim.

When you come out through the forest, the ground a mix of sand and dry brush, you see the mighty haraza tree for the first time. Its roots knuckle out of the soil fifty yards away, its branches reaching overhead farther still. The gnarled trunk sits like a giant on the ground, body seated and bent slightly forward, folds of bark bulging out like a belly, legs resting half in the earth. You do not try to shoot up into its branches, the branches so tall, so thick, so far away, a projected stone could barely reach. And there is a silence the leaves seem to speak—the millions of leaves—that draws you into a silence of your own. You walk underneath its shade for minutes, walk until you come out to the other edge, the riverbed of the empty river, filled only in rainy season months.

Here, the red hull of a boat lies abandoned—used only when the water comes, pushed out to ferry those not knowing how to swim to the other side, to the villages some distance away. Villages on the other side of the river, away from Ati and its market and the streets you know. Your own world within a larger one, of which you know so little and can hardly take in more.

The riverbed now dry, you watch trains of donkeys packed with firewood or grass mats shuttle across the sandy bed to the market stalls a mile downstream, where thousands gather on market day, a Sunday, from the surrounding villages, from the entire prefecture.

The other way, to the right—upstream—the dry brush, the shrubs give way to knobby hills and dips in the gray earth, where mounds of brick kilns, like kingly tombs speckle the land. Men, pant legs rolled up to knees, and shirts unbuttoned or else taken off, sweat and labor in the sun, shoveling the earth from the holes they bear into it, forcing soil into molds, baking them in the furnaces that glow when the sun goes down.

That day you went hunting with a slingshot, that day you wandered through the trees and were awed by the myth of their roots and the riverbed they reached into, that day you came back with no struck game to show of—that day only the smart, calculating Atayib brought home a kill, sneaking beneath the tree where birds slept silently, marking the one he wanted before firing the spot-on pebble. You shot after birds the size of your thumb, and claimed none, but returned with so many memories.

Before the shoots spring into stems, before the rainy season runoff carves new dips and furrows in the road that runs around your neighbor's wall and the alleyway nearby, before all this you join the children moving like a pack around the nearly deflated green rubber ball, barely larger than your fist. The feet tangle together as each tries to thrust his or her way to the ball, to corral it out and toward the two round trunks acting as goalposts. There is Atayib, laughing as another steals the ball out from under him and sprints forward, skipping the ball across the sand until it passes past the trees. "Kushuk!" Atayib yells out as the other children whoop. He breaks out into his favorite song—*Comment tu t'appelle . . . Je m'appelle . . . Coupé, coupé bibamba . .*

Your brother disappears, brings out the Franklin gray ball you had brought with you from America. Your friends whoop louder at the sight of the untouched rubber, bereft of thorns and scuffs from rocks, the ball's inner bladder inflated to bursting. The ball drops into the midst of the soccer players, and the scramble begins with heightened fury. You are so slow you can't even come close to where the ball is pounded with stronger legs. Pow! A boy, Abdel-Aziz, steps away for a second, shaking off the sting on his shin from where the ball had struck.

And then suddenly it is just you facing Abakar, the ball at his feet, dancing around it like a figure skater. He then sizes the goal up, behind you some ten yards, before he smashes the ball up and into your face. The sky reels, trees clouding over, and for a second your brain resets as a television screen does when power is cut and then restored. Your eyes open to eyes ringing around you where the treetops had been, staring at you with curiosity, before you're helped to your feet as you shake out the rattling in your mind. You try and keep playing, the fury restored once more after the brief delay, but you have to leave the crowd, brain swimming, and walk down the path to your blue gate, which you enter, greeting Moussa who sees you blink and tip your head down as if expecting the earth to open its mouth and swallow. The only thing that lessens the throb is the foam mattress on your newly varnished bed, the one the construction crew from the south had come and crafted, sanding and planing its slats to Gambai songs before calling you *da boi* and telling you to *amman mai*, which you'd obligingly do—the water swishing from the cup you'd hand to the one who'd asked.

Before you grow into a teenager, into the years you wrestle with your difference between your white skin and those around you, how you would always be 'other'—nasara, ameriki. Before your own struggle would sometimes keep you days inside, waiting selfishly for your friends to meet you in your yard, rather than going out to find them. Before you became afraid of what the neighborhood kids might call you, might remind you of what you were, what you are . . .

Before all this—you are a child yourself, unknowing and uncaring, wanting only a touch of the soccer ball.

When the day cooled and Ati woke up from its hours-long siesta in hot sun heat, your yard would fill with friends come to pound the basketball across the square space of yard. First, Al Goni in slacks and school uniform, shirt taken off to reveal his Denver Nuggets jersey, which you had purchased in a sports store in some Denver suburb, your family on vacation and you recognizing the name of the player you both loved—Boykins. The tiny, pestering player you would watch and marvel at. Small figure darting between the larger players, nailing a shot when given a sliver of space.

Al Goni would come with his brother, Bichara, talking as he dribbled through his legs about English proverbs he learned in school. *Make new friends but keep the old.* Feet planted, ball drawn up above his head, then swish. *One is silver the other is gold.* And Atayib, the tallest of all your friends, son of the lean farmer with the goiter in his neck you knew not to stare at. Atayib, always with the smile, even as he told you, years later when you were men, that his newborn infant, born to his newly wedded wife, had returned to the earth he came from.

And Abba Noh, gold tooth from where his original had been cracked from a fight. You were at first enemies, your teams colliding like titans on the basketball court at the town's outskirts, where herds of cattle came in, framing the lone court in a sphere of dust. You battled together in the leagues your brother started, talent quickly surpassing your own—the Arab street children living by this re-poured court, learning how to do a crossover in a day, learning how to play off the right hand or left, drive to the hoop, switching hands mid-second to take it up left or right of rim. Your teams—Excellence, Celtics, Explosif—all failed before the wonder of Abba Noh's Lakers, his teammates so tall they towered over you, muscles so thick you wondered how they still fell into the age group of the youth league. So tall they must have been born from their mothers as grown men.

One championship game you thought you had them, up some points with minutes left. Then, the Lakers started raining threes, Abba Noh pulling up well behind the three-point line. When, seconds left, you had the final shot, drawing the team to a time out, you inbounded the ball, ran around your teammate to receive it at the top of the key, lifting up a shot that rolled around the outside of the rim and missed. Your face must have been soaked red from the rivalry that seethed within your fourteen-year-old veins as the onlookers flooded the court, whooping and holding up the Lakers players as champions.

But you would grow out of it, this swelling, hormonal anger. You and Abba Noh would grow to sit as high-schoolers reading sports magazines at sunset. You would grow so that you played cards together at his family's house, biscuit tray with tea glasses and thermos brought in by his mother, wrapped in swirling orange lafiyes and arms jangling gold bracelets, the wise woman who would become the town's first female mayor. You would grow so that as you and Abba Noh became men, your bodies not yet filled out, you chased him around the court and laughed as he faded away and swished the ball yet again in your face.

Ramadan would not stop your games. As the boys began fasting, another attempt at becoming men, the games started later, the boys weaker—and you took advantage of the fact that you didn't fast. But still the games lasted until the muezzin called at maghrib, and then Bichara and your other friends would rush to the clay water duané, cooling at the base of the hajlij tree, take the plastic cup and scoop from the darkness and drink, eyes closed as water dripped down on shirts, speckled the sand, but they were too thirsty to care.

You remember one of the early days your friends gathered for basketball, the teams quickly set—brothers versus brothers, you and Bentley against Bichara and Al Goni. The 4 p.m. sun drew gold shapes along the cream wall, paint peeling after rainy season downpours. But your skin was heated not from the emerging sun's rays but from something within. After all, these early teen years were the years you felt a choice within you every hour—when your teenage temper flared at the smallest thing: a missed shot, a few teasing words, any suggestion that you weren't what you thought yourself to be.

So when the game wasn't going well for you, and Bichara and Al Goni wound around you, laughing at the joy of the game and the swished net and the ball pounding away the dirt at your feet—when you saw all this, you lunged for the ball when it was in Al Goni's hands, his back turned to you. His frame, half your size, lurched forward at the contact. The ball, dislodged from too strong a hand, sailing upward and ramming his chin. You took two steps and realized what you'd done—your gentle friend, Al Goni who said all words with a grin, who speculated about the world more than you did, was hurt, his eyes filling with tears. Tears more for what a friend had done to him and less for the dull throb of pain coming from his jaw. Bichara came close to his younger brother, wrapped him in his arms, and together they said a quick good-bye. Rushing out the blue gate in silence, leaving you to study the yard they'd filled with laughter and now left a void.

"Why would you do that?" your own brother was asking you. "Couldn't you see that was way out of line?" Bentley dropped the ball he had picked up and let it roll away to the bushes along the wall. You shook your head, knew any answer couldn't excuse the fury you had embarrassed yourself with.

You turned and walked into the unlit living room of your house, past the dining table, and into the dark of your room. The hot tears came then—grief you felt for having lost a friend because of your own teenage emotions. Grief for the things you always tried your hand at but came up empty—always at a loss despite the good you longed for beyond you.

But the next afternoon came and Al Goni and Bichara were in the yard. You were not ready for the smiles they displayed, faces bright with forgiveness, with a willingness to forget and act as if nothing had ever happened. You fumbled a few words of apology, and they laughed along with you, taking up the ball in their hands to start a new game.

The hours with them that stretched over the coming years is time you cannot explain. Countless afternoons spent lounging around drinking mango juice—your hands dropping in the thinly sliced pulp onto the blender's blades, scooping heaps of sugars and clattering cubes of ice down into the glass container. Bichara would eventually leave for schooling in Burkina, and Al Goni would follow in his wake several years later—but before all the departures, before the uncertain years where tomorrows hung in the balance like suspended suns over the horizon, you would experience friendship as you never had before and never will since—hours you spent watching *Lord of the Rings* together, you translating into Arabic an imagination your teenage minds all drank in. Staying up in the evening to watch the inauguration of Obama—Al Goni and Bichara having captured the same hope of a country half a world away. Speculating together about the war rumors that rose and flared every three months. Rumors that would one day cease to be rumors, becoming reality breathed across your safe borders.

There were nights you would leave their house, the moon so bright you could see every person walking the street all the way down, and the two brothers would walk with you. Not content for just having hosted you, but considering it their duty to make sure you found your own door. The close-walled houses framing their street opened up onto school grounds which you traversed in the dark, the sound of three pairs of sandals sifting sand like the whispers coming from the wind-filled tree leaves nearby. You would gaze up at the stars, aware of their permanence, yet hardly aware of the impermanence of these night walks beneath them.

"Sleep well," the brothers would say, and you would shake their hands, teeth flashing in the light of the moon. Then, their two figures would melt away into the night, down the main road until the shadows of the giant trees blocked out the night, eclipsing the moon's rays until the two brothers were consumed.

Some nights when the skies clear of dust, when the clouds finally empty themselves over the cracked land, you bring out the slender tube of a telescope, perch it in the center of your yard, and put an eye to the eyepiece. The fluorescent bulbs hanging from the walls have been shut off, the bugs no longer dinging against glass. The only light of the city comes from pockets of electricity scattered many doors down in a few directions, the rumble of generators supplying power for just a few more hours. Still, the darkness is unfathomable—and as your eye adjusts the stars number the black so much they are like letters on a page, a page that can be studied, yes, but not comprehended.

You train your telescope to the flash of star just over the northeast corner of your yard. There, through the lens, is a nebula burning constant, multicolored light revolving around itself in harmony, balls of blue and green and red flame swirling into a circle you stare into. When later you read Dante in college, come across the climax of the pilgrim arriving at Empyrean, when he gazes at the Trinity and speech fails him, you picture in your mind this nebula. Of course there are no words.

You find Mars, burning like matchflame against the dark. You stare at Saturn, too, ring fixed saucer-like, frozen by millions of miles and an old telescope lens. But always you finish by training the telescope back to the nebula, back to the revolving orbs of light.

When the sheikhs bring in their clansmen, the men ride through with pride, swords belted to their flowing captaniyes or held aloft and shaken with defiance, horses snorting and kicking up the sand of Chari Kabir with high steps.

In between them, the city boys speed their Yamaha motorcycles or Yamaha-knock-offs, weaving through the dust clouds to the large parade grounds that can be seen from your front door, where lines of hundreds of women twirl their braids to the beat of the nougara, deep-sounding with high taps blistering at millisecond rhythms. The primary and secondary students march down holding the flag and singing the songs they have been practicing up until this day, the day the president flies in and greets his people. *Lève les yeux, l'avenir est à toi.* All are migrating to the parade grounds, which fill with the light and lines of men and women, clusters of children darting to and fro, and the beige military trucks full of soldiers turbaned in camo, studying the crowds for suspicious activity.

Your brother is there at the roundpoint outside of the governor's house, at the painting of the president your Arabic teacher, Oustaz Boukhari, painted, with President Deby's face solemnly foregrounded against a backdrop of paved roads, skyscrapers, and military jets. When the president alights from a white truck that had sped fast through the crowd, he surveys the masses, no doubt picking your brother's white face out in the crowd, before he says, in a voice the people hush to hear, "Leleku"—some polluted version of Arabic greeting, a diluted pidgin vocabulary used everywhere in the capital that the rest of the country acknowledges with a laugh, and here the street children giggle around Deby and the adults wonder why their president would use the kind of word an N'Djamena grandmother might use.

Those years, when the campaign printed out flyers and the ballot boxes were filled with re-election ballots for the president (or if not filled, emptied and replaced), those years evaporate like the Batha in September, when the water ceases to rain and stream down from its source in Balala land. You remember the first year you moved out to Ati—discovered that the far guestroom at the yard's edge was filled with a foot of campaign materials the neighbors would later use as toilet paper. You remember the elections and the rumors, how a single town of five hundred could churn out two thousand votes for Deby. How soldiers would appear in the night at polling stations, empty the boxes of their contents, and change any contrary votes to those for the national party—*Movement Patriotique du Salut,* Patriotic Movement of Salvation. How those in opposition would risk life and limb to vote otherwise and would devise creative ways of slipping in an opposing vote into the ballot box between two

Deby vote cards (which were skillfully slipped back up into a shirt sleeve or a fold of the lafiye).

And you remember your last two years there—the speeding train of Hummers that came through, unannounced, each chrome hull painted a different hue. Your friends would tell you, "That was just the president." And when you asked why there were so many cars for just one man, they said, "He doesn't want his enemies to know which one he rides in. So if there was ever an attempt on his life, they'd have to guess."

But still the people would find reason to celebrate, reason for the Arab leaders to come in from the outlying villages with their horses and best-dressed men. And it was one of these days, your father driving several friends and you out for a visit elsewhere in the town, when the motorcycle of a city boy came whirring around your truck, and in the thick cloud of dust, struck a child crossing the street. And your father slammed the brakes, and you all got out and he picked up the girl out of the sand, checked her bones for breaks, and carried her to the truck, sped to the hospital, and you stayed behind, plans changed, to watch the taillights disappear in the kicked up sand.

Sometimes you are on a road that twists its two tire tracks around knife-tipped bushes. Othertimes the road straightens across the endless nagga, the packed-dirt plain, where you can see the figure of a farmer from two miles away, arms balancing a rusted hoe atop his shoulder. Above him, a starling murmuration spreads then twists against a backdrop of azure sky. Each year, the road changes. Each year, the road is determined by the Land Cruisers and market lorries that navigate it, plowing through sand in the wake of the rainy season, when all tire tracks disappear from earth.

In the first few years, the tracks took you by a small village, unique in that several old colonial buildings loomed half-abandoned by the side of the road, rising from the midst of several thatched huts and millet stalk walls. The first times you drove through with your family, you thought it odd, curious, but didn't know why the place seemed hardly alive, the few villagers you'd see, walking slowly out to a well or pausing from work to watch your truck speed by on the desert road.

It was in those first few months, after moving from capital to small town, a Swiss woman arrived at your doorstep, directed there because your family was the only white family for hundreds of miles, and people assumed you'd know her. And you did, your parents having met her at some point, somewhere. She was traveling around for a Red Cross project, and when she began to speak of a small leprosy village on the road to Ati, the old French clinic buildings baked to death in the Sahel sun, you knew exactly the place she was telling you.

You thought leprosy was something you read about in the Bible, some mythic affliction washed clean in divine rivers. You didn't know that others still walked with the disease eating away at their flesh. That the veiled villagers gazing at passing cars from behind half thatch walls were covering more than just skin.

Some years later, your family on another cross-country trip, you waited in the car while your father bargained for roadside grilled meat. A woman, wrapped in a faded lafiye, her face folded by years of sun, begged for change at the window your father left cracked. When she raised her hand to tap on the glass, you could see her speckled flesh, her missing fingers.

You and your brother drive north with friends, the dry brushlands transitioning to dips of sand and rut, the trees growing fewer, until they twist up out of the ground, petrified like bone. At the old colonial outpost, the place a French company came in and herded goats into tin roof barns and made goat cheese, you get out and stretch your legs, and Abakar speaks with a family that lives in the abandoned hulk of factory. The children come out to see this curious truck full of townspeople and two white teenagers. "You are not far from Sarihat," their teenage son tells you, one arm akimbo and the other waving north. "Maybe an hour more. Watch for where the camels gather thickest."

You continue on, the road getting sandier, more difficult for the tires to tread. The sun begins to lay down in the horizon, and you worry about finding your way through the desert in the dark.

But then you see the camel herd, the circle of nomad tents stretching far around, and the crowd of people clapping, ululating—the men in their finest embroidered captaniyes, the groom, Ali, in his grand boubou made just for the day. And as you and your brother and friends get out, you are swept up in the crowd. "Take a picture of us!" several faces around you ask, and you are turning in every direction, framing then focusing on smiling faces, white teeth cleaned by neem tree branches glinting in the evening light. Members of the groom's family jump into view. Boys you played with on the sandy basketball court in quartier Arabe, boys now lengthening like the shadows stretching out from the nearby acacia trees.

When next you look up, your brother is riding with two friends atop a camel, the camel joining with several others to trot off around the camp and back. The camels approach you again, the young men on their beasts' backs raise their swords high, look fierce for as long as they can before breaking into laughter. Abakar asks you, "Haroun, why don't you ride as well?" And for a second you feel fifteen pairs of eyes circle around you, excited for another white boy to climb up a camel's back, parade around. You feel the thrill within you, the rush of the lurch backward and up as the camel stands. But you shake your head, wave off their request, "It's not important," you mumble. "Ma muhim, he says!" Abakar laughs.

You do not want the lens to focus on you. You feel already as if you have encroached upon the space of others, as if you have hijacked the wedding of a friend you and your brother have grown up with, battled at basketball with. In trying to avoid the lens, you only focus it more—your friends laugh, but are confused. Why wouldn't you want to ride in the dying light? Why wouldn't you want to shake a sword at the sky?

That night, the noise quiets down, and the visiting men all lie out on mats strewn out across the gesh. Abakar is telling a story of the spirit men who follow you at night, wanting to drive you past the town's furthest building and into the desert to claim you. Then, he describes the rumors of the woman in Abeche, the woman with a feather moustache, who fathered children with other women. And those around you who are still awake click their tongues, shake their heads in wonder.

When your brother and several others decide to walk out to relieve themselves, a wedding tradition, you join them, the sound of your sandals like millet grain tossed across the surface of a metal sufra. The men squat, letting their captaniyes shield them as they urinate, but in your own captaniye you do not know yet how to master this maneuver, so you stand awkwardly, embarrassingly, untying the drawstring of the pants beneath the fabric folds before watching your urine stream out into the night, to the dirt below that bubbles and foams.

The moon is full, all of you are in a line, and only you are standing, and you can feel the smirks of the men to your left. But no one chooses to say anything. Your way back to the sleeping mats is slower, your friends talking about the camels that sleep standing or folded up on the ground, slumbering bodies that stretch out as far as the eyes can see. "Seven hundred head of camel," Mahamat Saleh speaks, voice low with awe.

In the morning, you go to the groom's father's tent, he has invited the two white brothers for tea, and he welcomes you with a grin that lifts his gray-tinted beard, the dimpled skin parting the weathered cracks that have been exposed to sun and wind for sixty years. He makes sure you have a small plate of peanuts before he steps out, pulling apart the curtain of his tent, to bring in the tea kettle from outside. A son brings a bowl of camel milk, and the father mixes them. "Have you had diarrhea yet?" the old man chuckles as he pours you cream tea into small glasses, the steam lifting and getting shot through with rays coming from a crack in the curtain doorway. "A few more days of drinking tea with camel's milk, and you'll really be struggling!"

After the laughter dies down, he then asks about your father, the daktor, and thanks you for coming to the wedding. Mahamat Saleh, Tahir, and his other sons gather on the next rug over, and you play what feels like is the thousandth game of basara since you've arrived. Searching for the two of clubs, the aces, and not finding them. Getting a jack to sweep the deck, exposing your adversary's final card, but no card to match it, no basara. The cards are cleared from the grass mat surface, and you all lazily lean back and ramble on in slurred early afternoon conversation as flies buzz around your faces, trying to find a place to land. One by one, friends drop off into slumber.

And then it is time for you to leave, for the green truck to shudder south, to follow the tracks toward town before the light grows too dim to see. The family gathers—the bride and groom long since disappeared—and they wish you and your family well. Abakar guides the truck across the winding tracks, across the plain where only hooves mark out a path, and past the tin roofs and silos of the cheese factory, before the tracks become a rutted road, and the desert becomes a town and a street and a blue gate, where you and your brother enter, and lie down to sleep off the desert heat and the camel milk and the cracked lips on both your faces from drinking the rationed amount of a nomad.

When you wake, it is almost night. You try to tell your mother, your father, about all you'd seen, but you find it difficult to place the camel races and the milk-filled bowl into coherent words. Your mind still water-starved, you go to bed, and wake the next day as if the world had never noticed you were gone. The day is filled with all the normal things—school, lunch, friends coming over to bounce the basketball in the afternoon, and your father's small gatherings of middle-aged men drinking tea in the shade of the yard's corner. It was almost as if you had never driven into the desert. If only your skin wasn't baked the color of the earth, the color of slumbering camels.

The two brothers, Al Goni and Bichara, come to you, saying the mother of Mahamat Saleh and his brothers has passed away suddenly, and they are gathering to mourn her loss at the house by the basketball court and athletic grounds, the wide mud door that opens to a plain of dirt and athletes. You put on your best, a polo and khakis, and walk with your friends to the funeral. When you arrive, a number of men are scattered on a three-piece mat spread out under the central tree, but Al Goni and Bichara tell you to follow them deeper into the yard, to a house where Mahamat Saleh and his brothers mourn together. You sit in the corner of the mud-walled room and study the whispering faces of those you know and those you don't. Boys you once laughed with on the basketball court at the end of day—now boys you'd walk with to the fields and forests, skipping stones. Boys you'd read newspapers with under the shade of a tree at the day's hottest moment, discuss Chadian politics together, speculate about the latest telenovela playing at the nearby theater, predict the success (and failures) of Brazil or Argentina or France at the upcoming World Cup.

Now, these boys are muttering to themselves, prayer beads gliding through fingers—and you realize the half-spoken words are the names of God, chanted in unison. An hour passes as you watch and wonder. Then, a young man parts the thin curtain covering the doorway, clouds the light for a second with his frame, and asks, "How many?"

And each group, each small huddle of three or four souls, tallies up the names they have counted on scraps of paper, lifting each number up to the young man at the doorway, who in a flash of light you see is your friend, Mahamat Saleh, whose mother has just passed. He adds the numbers in his head. "Four thousand." And walks out to the faki at the base of the tree outside, where the father, now widowed, waits with the rest of the family and the other old men of the quartier.

On the walk back home, you ask why the names were counted. "To tip the scales in her favor," replies Bichara. "To give her one last chance to enter the kingdom of heaven."

When you went out to the Batha with your friends, your angular bodies on the knife-edge of adulthood, when you bent low and sifted through the sand with your fingers, when you found the smoothest stone, flat like the abandoned hub caps lying in the mogoff, did you know that when each of you threw these stones, watching them skip, that the stones could not stay in air much longer? Did you know that soon each stone would have to splash then sink? Did you know that one by one each of you standing by the riverbed would disappear and reappear across some faraway border? That each of you would send a new message, like a stone, coming across a twelve-digit number—It's me. It's Al Goni or Greet for me your family or Ya mawadir, where have you gone?

Did you know that long after the bullets found their home in the ground and the bodies were cleaned up from the streets, that only the river would remain, filling in rainy season just like it always has been, rushing downstream just as it always will be?

Crimson jerseys race like wraiths in the dying sunlight, the gold and grit of light catching airborne sand, making the field and its players glow. You spot Abba Noh, waving for the ball on the wing, watch as the ball skids across the dirt to his cleated feet which dance around it, defenders jabbing and chasing. When he lays the ball off for a teammate who skies it high over the goal, the crowd around you laughs and the children whoop as the team retreats back for the goal kick to come.

There is no need for any line to be painted in the sand—the field is bordered by bodies, the men of the town just off from work and their young boys. Schoolgirls jostle at the corners to catch a glimpse, and the mothers of the players are scattered throughout, lifting encouraging words to their sons, the women who mutter to themselves when they see their sons go down—*la'illah*. With every move of the ball, every effort of each player, there's a chorus of chants from the sidelines: "pass" when a player has held on too long; "merci" when a defender has been thwarted or a cross has been made; "yallah—frappe!" when a player has the ball at the top of the box and the goal is in sight, the keeper crouching for the expected shot. When finally there is a goal, the children lead the charge across the field, leaping and throwing up their arms, and the men stride forward with a shake of the fist and a handshake with the nearest player. The opposing team, dejected, stares at the place the ball has gone.

In the setting light, you see the flash of Abba Noh's gold tooth, watch as his team is finally bested, and the score is knotted 1–1. The whistle blows minutes later, and again the crowd rushes in, framing the 18-yard box, as players line up to take their chances in a penalty shootout. First, Abderrazak lines up a drive to the top left corner. Then, Hamid chips it wisely over the keeper in response. Abdel-Aziz peeters out a shot straight into the keeper's hands, and Djiddo responds with a shot so hard the keeper can't keep it out though he puts a hand on it. Another player hits a post, the pressure too great, so that by the time Abba Noh steps up to the spot, the game is on the line. With the crowd finally quiet, quiet to the point where it seems the only living thing is the body of the red jersey standing at the top of the box, you watch your friend stride forward and smash it straight into the top right corner, and the children leap up again shouting, "Coupe! Coupe! Coupe!" And the players surround him, embracing him as they jump up and down, chanting a song that the surrounding supporters pick up and spread through the multitude. When a metal trophy is produced, its veneered finish scratched and worn so that the faux-silver reveals the brass beneath, you watch as the team lifts it high over their heads as fans take pictures with their cell phones, the throng migrating over to the sea of motorcycles and pickups that will parade them around town, horns honking and fists upraised.

When you go to sleep that night, your dreams will be of the kicked-up dust and the soaring ball. You will see Abba Noh, and the others you recognize and know, jumping in the light, the sun barely visible over the tall neem trees at the edge of the parade platform. You will hear the children chanting the names of your friends, and you will see the small boys attempt the same tricks with tiny rubber balls or wads of paper at their feet, rolling the ball sideways and sidestepping before bringing it back around for a hit on the outside of the foot, the ball lifting then spinning right. You will dream of the soaring ball again. You will watch it continue in the air, lifting and turning like a globe as its trajectory lifts up, up, up. When it reaches the net, it will pass through a hole, so that it keeps going, keeps lifting. You will not cease to have this dream.

In the twilight night, you go out to the brickyards. In the twilight night, you walk beyond the crashed Libyan plane. In the twilight night, you see the horserace through the trees, men in white captaniyes spectering forward on Arabian horses, tails arched, necks extended. In the twilight night, you watch your brother dip into the rahad with the others. In the twilight night, you go out beyond to the Batha, skip stones with friends across the surface, watch as every skip of theirs matches your own stone that plops quickly in. In the twilight night, Moussa's son is born. In the twilight night, Moussa's son fades away. In the twilight night, Moussa dreams a dream of a cat jumping on his head and smothering him in urine. In the twilight night, Moussa takes sick, nearly dies as the IV drips. In the twilight night, they shuttle Moussa to the capital. In the twilight night, they perform surgery on an intestinal hole. In the twilight night, Moussa sits up, face radiant, walks out of the hospital room.

In the twilight night, the herds of cattle low at the outskirts of town. In the twilight night, each cow enters town, then breaks off from the others, finding its home door. In the twilight night, the dusk and dust, kicked up from the cows, hovers like fog. In the twilight night, the shadow of a man and a motorcycle merge into the vague horizon.

In the twilight night, Brahim is making his tea, sprinkling in perfume drops to make it smell like Europe. In the twilight night, the women and the children surround a small bowl of sauce. In the twilight night, the beggar, belly distended, sings his song at the gate. In the twilight night, you go out on the street, look up and see the star clouds, every single pinprick of light, see the nebula flashing blue, green, red with the naked eye.

In the twilight night, you are no longer there.

A woman holds your hand, shakes it vigorously, her old folded skin crisp and calloused to the touch. "Mabrouk!" she exclaims and you thank her, leaving the small naming ceremony behind. You had woken in the thin stream of dawn, woken and walked out to Chari Kabir, the sunlight shining from all the way down, illuminating the tips of the neems, the tiny roundabout (broken from a midnight truck), and the shiny surfaces of what must be trash scattered around the entrance to the market. You had entered the neighbor's yard, the place where Moussa was celebrating the birth of his son and the naming of him, and had chosen to name him after you—*Haroun.* You sipped coffee from clear glasses, sat and joked around with your friends as you all blinked away sleep. Moussa's voice rasped when he told you of the honor, and you didn't know what to say besides a small, inadequate shukran that seemed to come from somewhere far down the alley behind you. Then the men quieted, the faki at the center raised his upward palms, prayed, then whispered with Moussa for a minute, before the new name was made official—Haroun, scattering like wind-swept twig-leaves from ear to ear. One by one, they looked at you, your friends and neighbors, your father and his old man friends, and they too blessed you, congratulated you with mabrouks.

When you walked away and the last woman blessed you, when you entered your house again and started your schooling, did you know the boy would not live another month? Did you know that you would ask Moussa by the gate one day about your namesake, to hear about his health, only for the father to reply that his child has returned? From the other side of the gate, you heard a small gathering of swallows twip and call before they lifted out of the tree growing from gutter sewage, the birds beating their wings and rising up to the nearby neem trees by the road, joining the bigger flock, those already there making room for them.

You arrive at Hissein's for his Saturday afternoon English lesson—join him on the bench outside his one room house then mark up the wobbly blackboard. *What will you buy at the market today? How many brothers and sisters do you have?* When the lesson ends, Hissein brings out a pack of playing cards, and a sister sets down a coffee thermos and glass funjal, which you cloud with chalky fingerprints as cardamom and ginger burn your throat all the way down. Your brain awake with caffeine, the two of you begin hours-long conversation, lasting until the maghrib call. Will the rebels ever go away? Will the rebels turn out to be good people? Will the president deliver on his promise to bring a paved road to Ati, to finally send electricity through the abandoned wires hanging from street poles like forgotten campaign decorations? At some point, you migrate inside to sit on the rug, talking more politics—how the teachers haven't been paid or how the country has crawled itself out of war or found itself in another one, and how everyone is tired, so tired. Between Hissein's words, you start to wonder—before accountability, before corruption can be done away with, there must be peace, peace that brings end to the war between bodies, end to the war of the mind. Peace that means compromise, that means overcoming a reluctance to look past daily infractions so long as lives are no longer lost. Is this the reason why so many have been content with a president entirely corrupt, who keeps the country frozen for two decades but has at least stopped the bullets from raining?

Othertimes, Hissein asks what your other country is like—your American home—what the people are like, if it is really like in the movies with the gangs and the cops and the pristine romances, and if there really are *americain noirs* whose skin has the same richness as his? Is there crime there, and surely are there no rebels or do the schools close for lack of pay and is it not hard to visit this country? You reply that yes it is all like this, but maybe not as much as in the movies, or maybe just different. You don't know how to translate another world into Arabic, another world with its own problems and politics, what your relatives worry about each day. It is a different frame of mind, a different state you enter into after plane flights and airport stays. One life lived here and one life lived there. It is a world that does not reach across the ocean except in you, and likewise when you will leave this place, when you will leave these conversations and coffee cups by the blackboard with Hissein, you will carry all this back with you the same way. A vessel of worlds, vessel of memory.

With Hissein, you sometimes engage in neighborhood gossip—which family is sending which father to prison to get sobered up, which child is being sent to N'Djamena for his formal education so that one day he can take care of his siblings and parents, which friend of yours has disappeared years before and turned up on the eastern front in a uniform and which side he has chosen to fight for. You talk about the boy who was too young to ride a motorcycle but still did and wrecked it. You talk about the bus passenger who stuck his head out the window, whose face was shorn off by an oncoming car. And you talk about the cell phone shack on the street corner, how they are now using cell phone credit between cities to deposit and transfer money, how this is all such an innovative solution to the bags of money people usually carry in trucks across the country, hoping they are never asked what's in them by greedy police, who always make passengers exit and empty their bags on the roadside.

Always, Hissein brings out a stack of clothes to iron and fold as he talks, and you watch as he takes a shirt or a pair of pants and spreads it out on the rug with his only good arm—the other curled against his chest, half the size, twisted from a birth injury and the marabout who tied the bandage too tight. One day, Hissein tells you of this story. How he came out after his brother Hassan, and something was not right, and his mother lived for several more days until she died and was buried before the sun set.

It is never about how little English the two of you use—though Hissein works hard at it, crafting new words but always struggling with their unfamiliar shape, a struggle caused no doubt by your fumbling first foray into teaching. It was never about the English but for the real reason he invites you over: to sip gahawa together and philosophize, munching on Nigerian glucose biscuits. He asked for

English lessons but longed for friendship—the friendship of Saturday afternoons, a friendship that deepened with every empty funjal glass. Hissein with his maimed arm, you with your white skin—things that connect you so closely. You speak together until the dust-filled evening. You speak underneath the deep goldflecked cloud and removed moon, just a sliver over the horizon, coming from another world.

It is your senior year and you are in the capital, wary of the bullets you heard just months ago. You call up Hassan and Djiddo and decide it would be fun to visit the Kempinski, the luxury hotel funded by Libyan oil money in an effort to soothe old war wounds between the two neighboring nations. You want to walk around its glistening halls, flip-flops clacking on marble, hotel attendants eyeing you with suspicion. You ride the elevator to the top story with your friends, smile at each other in the gold panels of the elevator, making faces. The only elevator you ever rode in the whole country. At the top story, there is an empty restaurant space—chairs tacked against the wall and a carpet, royal purple, spread out across many spacious rooms. From the look of it, the restaurant has never been used, its design begun but abandoned prematurely. You walk by an oval mirror, rimmed with gold like sun rays reaching out, take a picture of your smiling faces framed within it. Then, your friends are by the floor-to-ceiling glass, looking down from the tallest point in the city, in the country. Only the tall Tibesti mountains are higher, but you will never see them, that land where nomad tribesmen live a perpetual rebellion.

Beyond the pristine lawns of the hotel grounds, the sprinklers spraying moisture disappearing into a cloud of evaporated mist, beyond the UN trucks lined up around the roundpoint checkered with the flags of Chad, Libya, France, and other nations—beyond all this you see the city, the sand-colored lots where mansions lie half-built before money ran out to finish them. You see the Palais du Peuple, the Chinese-constructed house of parliament, and its chandeliers gleaming through the massive tinted windows, and you wonder what the place looked like filled with looters and rebels two years before, during the first attack, when these outer limits of the city, these big-money projects, became the battlefields where tanks broke down gates and backed in, turrets aimed at street.

Only a couple blocks away, one of your father's colleagues came home to a terrible sight. Deciding to leave as war rumors swelled, he packed his family up and left town with their youngest son, the last of their children still at home, Alan, a friend of yours. In their wake just days later, a group of rebels broke in, chased by government soldiers unloading submachine gun clips at them. The walls were sprayed by bullets as the men sprinted around the house and hid in the back, under the porch swing or in the laundry bushel. The soldiers found them within seconds, dragged them out into the yard, and lined them up and shot them.

Alan showed you the bullet holes several months later when you visited, and you felt the holes with your fingertips, imagined running for your life as the thuds beat behind you, debris raining down on your head, your shoulders. "Could you imagine?" he asked. You thought then that you could, but when the shells poured out over the pavement two years later elsewhere in the city, and you were there to experience battle at its white hot center, you would come to realize what fleeing death really felt like.

And now you, standing in the luxury hotel, staring down at the war-ridden neighborhoods knowing not only recent months of violence but also intimating the baggage of decades, you make some comment about the war or the frozen development of the surrounding streets, and Hassan and Djiddo nod their heads and grow silent. You should have said something—anything—other than the vision that was right in front of them, the long slow waking nightmare.

In the music of memory there are discordant chords—not the chords of the afternoons you spend sitting on your floor, first strumming your brother's guitar. No, these are the false notes of life, played off-rhythm. Like the moment you heard that the tall boy you'd played against a few weeks before, Al-Wali, had found his father's pistol in the dash of his Land Cruiser. As he felt the cold steel in his hands, the gun went off inexplicably, shooting Al-Wali in the face, blood spraying window, steering wheel, seat.

Or the three children Ley told you about one day, after he had come in from the market. Three children in Quartier Sharrif who played with what they thought was a hard round ball but proved a grenade.

The discordant chord is played, its echo lingers, but it fades as memory's melody continues. As the music swells and swirls, if you listen closely, the off-note is still there, but veiled behind the larger music.

You hear the news standing in the kitchen—Moussa or Ley bringing it through the kitchen door—that the mighty haraza tree has fallen, that it had been struck by lightning, that its hulk and limbs now lie in piles, and that villagers and townspeople alike come and chop it up for firewood. You are sixteen, between the first rebel battle and the last, the two years when rumors spread like brushfire, when you don't know whether you will be staying or going each day. This is the time when your friends begin disappearing—heading off out of the country for schooling to places you need days on market trucks and buses to reach—Maroua, Maiduguri, Ouagadougou.

When you hear the news that the tree has fallen, you know the way in which you will remember the river shore will never be the same again. So you go out with your friends to mourn the tree's passing and come upon the huddled body of the giant tree, as if it has a weeping head bent down between its knees, as if it has been bloodied and bruised and is taking years to catch its breath before it grows up and out again. You take pictures of it, as if that will somehow help you stave off the loss, as if the broken roots and branches, piled prehistoric, will be given life when you later print them in full color and bleed. You walk among the fallen limbs, find a chipped piece of wood, and bring it home with you.

You still have it—a piece of the haraza tree. Sometimes you lay it out on your desk or let it rest in your palm. The oil of your fingers and the moisture of the air has yellowed the wood in the years that have passed. A relic to remind you of what was: that far-reaching tree, that mighty haraza with roots so deep they defied time.

You have been to heaven and back—the place under the gum tree and its shade, the taste of dates breaking apart on your tongue, the sight of tiny bits of mint leaves hovering in your tea. Heaven was the Madri smile, the Atayib laugh, the Hassan invite to come ride the motorcycle in the city streets, the bleat of taxis, the muezzin's call.

Heaven was the place where every flesh, every frame, every voice, every chuckle, every breath was filled with the twilight wind, with the raincloud shading over, with the first few drops of sweet water, washing all the dust from skin.

III
Atlanta
April 16, 2009

You wake in your brother's apartment in Atlanta. A single bulb in the hallway illuminates an open dryer and its door, and your brother is folding laundry and ironing a shirt for the trip. There is a steam-driven espresso machine shuddering on the kitchen counter, and you flick on the television and watch highlights of Big Baby Davis in a Celtics jersey sending a player to the floor as he sets a screen.

Together, you walk out with your bags, you and your brother, down the hill to the bus, which takes you to the MARTA station, the Saturday morning so early few join you on the platform. The train comes in, and you watch the old trees and colonial homes and redbrick restaurants and Chinese super buffets drift in and out of your train window vision. At the airport, your brother gets two espressos, walking gingerly through the traveling throngs with the tiny cups cradled in his fingers. Your plane lifts off with the smell of coffee beans in your nostrils, the two of you sitting together.

In the Canadian customs lane, you are pulled off to the side, separated from your brother.

"Why are you so young and traveling by yourself?" an official asks, darting her eyes between the passport and your face.

"I'm traveling with my brother, and I'm eighteen."

"Are you running away from home?" the woman asks.

Home. You want to laugh because this means so many things to you. That home is a place that can be abandoned, a place you can even outrun. Does home not always doggedly follow you, no matter how far you travel, no matter how hard you wrestle with the joys and pains of it? And yet you want to sink into a pained quiet for the same reason—what is home? Why would it ever be abandoned if found? And who is this person to ask such a difficult question, such a narrative-laced (and laden) question? So you choose the easy way out, the answer she is wanting: "I am here to visit the city and to go see my brother's film at the festival."

Next, a man goes through a series of questions as he unpacks each article of clothing stuffed in your roller carry-on. You watch as your dress shirts, underwear, books are stacked up on a metal table. Blue latex gloves rifle through your things, shoving socks and computer cords to the corners. There is nothing to be found because you are hiding nothing.

When you are released, the baggage claim doors slide open, and you see your brother standing with your host, the brother-in-law of Al Goni and Bichara. He remarks with a wry smile, "Haroun, what did you do wrong?" The music of his Arabic coming like a cool zephyr into the sterile baggage claim. And then you are riding in the back seat of his RAV4, his daughter chiming into the conversation next to you in her car seat, kicking up her shoes into the air, as the gray March sky hovers over Montreal. You see in her facial features the faint resemblance to your friends, the brothers, whose light skin, warm eyes, small button nose are always an inch away from mirth and dry wit.

As the tall glass buildings give way to immigrant streets, corner shop signs lettered with Arabic, your host stops by an ice cream store, gets out and brings back a cone for his daughter who happily slurps at it as you continue on your drive. You meet his wife at their apartment, Al Goni and Bichara's sister, AmHadji, and remember her from years ago, standing in your yard, trying the new words of English she had learned from a Peace Corps teacher. You talk and eat together as if you were thousands of miles across an ocean, dipping bread into a spicy moolah, letting the sting of shettah scratch your throat all the way down. But you are here in Canada, and as you eat, the flat screen against the wall plays a Canadiens hockey game, and your host gives a rundown of the team this season: "We have hopes of the playoffs this season. Just as long as we don't have more injuries. Tanguay will score his goals. Schneider will continue to be ageless."

When you used to talk soccer with your friends, a hundred miles south of the Sahara, did you ever think that one day you'd discuss hockey in Arabic over moolah and kissar, winter bent trees shuddering outside the window here in Canada?

The meal finished, you recline back. Reminisce about Ati, a world away from icy Montreal.

"Pictures!" AmHadji says, and her children gather around you and your brother on an embroidered mattress against the wall, their socks singing into the rug like the music of snow footfalls. The camera flashes and the digital image lights the face of the mother as she checks to see if it turned out well. She smiles and clicks in approval, holding the screen up to you and your brother. "It's good, isn't it?"

At the doorway, the children wave goodbye, and AmHadji promises to send you the photo. You walk down the stairs and out of the building, this small flat of home.

Then you are back in the car headed to a hotel downtown where the film festival screening your brother's film will begin. You wonder if Abakar will be there, if he has made it, but neither you nor your brother has received word if he has. Checked in, you lie down on your bed and doze off while your brother goes and finds him. And when you wake, Abakar is coming through the door, that same wide smile, kicked back head as if not a thing could come between him and his imagination, the same imagination that drove him to write script after script in tiny brown cahiers in between studying for exams or acting in the community troupe. After the three of you laugh and slap each other's hands in greeting, Abakar shakes out his new white shirt and tells you the story of buying it in a nearby store. "*Forty* dollars? Are all shirts in this world worth talata alif?"

Then, he begins to recount the journey of his flight from Cameroon—the place he'd been living in the last few months in the wake of the war fallout and the investigations to see who was sympathetic to the rebels. When he arrived at the Montreal airport, he walked up to the first official he saw and filed for political asylum.

The days go by quickly—you and your brother and Abakar walking through malls, flipping coins into fountains, and watching the copper coins sink. At the festival, you see films by other African directors flash by on the screen—a taxi driver in love and a man who has left home and tries to find his trafficked sister—and then there is Abakar's character on the screen, the boy-turned-soccer-player whose competitive edge drives him to insanity and a life spent abroad before he can return to his native land. At the awards ceremony, you film your brother and Abakar get up as their names are called for the mention d'honneur. Abakar unfolds a piece of paper, reads a short speech thanking the festival committee. "A big honor," he says. "My dreams are realized." You watch as a camera crew interviews them hours later. You are so far away from the dust-filled streets, from the games you all used to play and the old mini-cassette tape video cameras that blinked *Record* as the seconds ticked by.

When last you are together, you walk up to the small mountain just outside the city, to the wide stone expanse, the Chalet du Mont-Royal, and stare down at the skyline surrounding you. You wonder what Abakar is thinking, seeing something like this for the first time that isn't in a movie or a travel poster. Together you think about the way things were. The flashbulb illuminated theater skits they used to put on, Abakar with chalkdust in his hair to make him seem old. The time you filmed a movie scene out by the abandoned veterinary buildings by the river. The shaded street bench outside Madri's house where you could sit for hours and talk with everyone living around the block if you were there long enough, the sun fading from mid-afternoon to evening, the lights coming on one by one and the call from the nearby mosque guiding everyone inside to pray.

At checkout, you look down at the basket and the items your mother had sent you out to get—some milk, bread, eggs, cheese, coffee, and a snack or two—dark chocolate or biscuits. The euros start to add up, flashing green on the small cash register screen. You pay, bag your items, and walk out onto the street, office buildings and apartments crowding over the sand-speckled sidewalk, the quartz catching the light of the Parisian spring sun.

It had taken you longer to get groceries, after all. The bags of different bread, the multi-colored cereal boxes which ultimately you couldn't decide on. A thousand scents of cheese from the cheese aisle. These choices seem sin, standing in the aisles, staring at them. Excessive, given the heartpound of the journey from war to barracks to exile. Can you even call it exile—this wandering through Parisian streets, observing student protests on Thursday or bands of American tourists in Nikes and Yankee caps, groups you shirk away from, unknowing, not understanding?

The first real place you stayed—the first temporary home your family found after the evacuation—was a long-term residence inn in Noisy-le-Grand, a concrete-filled banlieue east of Paris. The lettering of the sign itself *Noisy Residence* descended vertically from the top of a five or six story tower, toward the mix of cement and redbrick that made the square look like some cross between a Russian Cold War housing project and a schoolyard. There were stairs up to its entrance, stairs also to the entrance of the mall, the *centre commercial*, that expanded out beneath the hotel.

And within this building—the green carpet, the rows and rows of doors down lengthy hallways—there was laughter, the laughter of children. Their parents working long hours at some other far reach of Paris, the girls and boys would filter out of their rooms, their French accents honed to perfection over their parents' Francophone ones. Not rolled *r*'s but the *r*'s that get caught up in your throat for a second before issuing from somewhere behind the tongue.

They were younger than you, these children, much younger, and when you walked out to the lobby to steal the wi-fi coming from the McDonald's downstairs, they'd crowd around your computer and comment on what you'd try to read, wanting you to turn on some cartoon or to play a song on YouTube.

You hardly ever took a turn around the mall beneath the hotel. Just a few times—not buying anything, of course, saving the few euros your parents would give you for metro tickets to see some other banlieue, to wander some other street where the scent of Algerian shawarma or Senegalese yassa hovered between the buildings.

One day you and your mother walked far to find a small guitar at a music store, a starter Takamine you struggled to justify spending the 70 euros to get. But together, you brought it home, your heart racing as you unzipped the bag for the first time, ran your fingers across its rosewood neck. You spent the next several months writing songs—about what it means to feel out of place, about the loss you felt, the friends left behind in another country rent by war. When it finally was time to head home, to pack up your belongings after months waiting to return—your mother took the guitar to a nearby music shop and sold it. There wasn't space to carry it on a flight to Tripoli and on to N'Djamena. And if you had found a way to check it, you'd almost certainly unzip it days later and find its body bashed in. Sometimes those songs you recorded with a cheap computer microphone, with a free recording program, come on when your music scrambles as it plays. Sometimes in the raw chords, your voice altogether cracking as it was beginning to form, you hear the chords of separation, what you will call, cautiously, the melody of exile.

You have returned with your mother and father, with your brother, and as you wake into your first day in the capital, you wake to the same buzzing moto, the same anxious honk and zoom of Peugeot taxi that once serenaded your life. When all of you are awake—dressed and ready—you drive around the city, and you are surprised at all that you see— the miles and miles of tin walls framing new multi-million dollar hotels, and the new Place du Peuple, where green grass stretches on for half a mile under pillars and archways praising the victories of the government. This was not at all how you remembered it. There were entire neighborhoods here—leveled in the wake of the attack as the government went house to house and "eliminated" those they thought were rebels, those who had melted away when the cause was lost, buried their uniforms to become citizens again. No, this was not at all how you remembered it. The smoke billowed from this place when the rebels had the palace surrounded, when the explosive-rigged buildings went off one by one, and the French gunships swooped in, emptying their clips on the villagers attempting to oust a propped-up leader.

As your family drives around, you are in awe of all the change—N'Djamena becoming a modern city finally, years later. But you are also angry, angry as if everyone is forgetting. As if every cement patch that filled in a bullet hole, every tin wall that hid rubble behind it, somehow lulls the city into a lotus silence, when in your mind, though years later, the battle still rages, the helicopter rotors still beat with annihilating precision.

And then you are taken past the first road bypass, the bridge that spans a roundpoint, and you all shudder—and laugh— never seeing anything like it before, a paved road rising over one of the worst gridlocked roundpoints in the city. Above, you look up and see the Libyan Hotel, the Kempinski, rising a stone's throw away, and the truck you are in pulls through the hotel's gate once more, and your family walks in, sits in its coffee shop that didn't exist before—a coffee shop in your country!—and it is then your brother nods, gets your attention, and you follow his gaze to watch Hassan walk in, a few years older, a few more gray hairs added to his head, the reason why he is called *abouchiebe*, father of age. You sit down together and order tea, the first glasses you will share with a friend once again in your country. For the first time you discover how hard it is to summarize your life, the life you've spent away—and you mumble through everything: college, marriage, job, grad school. You realize the hole you've felt despite everything, yet you realize life's trajectory, how a severance happens, a departure, and life vectors onward away from some parallel world you are from—how this parallel world grows too, changes and modernizes, and yet somehow everything, even you, remains the same at the core. You laugh yourself into a silence with them—your brother, your Chadian brother—and there is a moment when none of you knows what to say, so you sit together, stare at the carpet, stare back at each other, and smile.

Atayib beams at the doorway to his concession yard. He is taller if only for the confidence that runs through his shoulders down to his sandaled feet. A white captaniye, pristine, flows over his body as if a robe of kings.

"Fadal, my brother," he beckons to you, into the yard, past the neighbors' houses to his own in the corner, where a young woman beats a hardened lump of sugar as tea boils over a charcoal brazier.

"My wife," he says, and you greet her, and she smiles staring past you as is the custom, to not make eye contact with people of the opposite sex. Somehow in the way she smiles, in the way she labors over the tea, in the way her husband lingers before he turns into the house—you sense a close love that binds them, some power born past fire and shadow. Glowing coals in a brazier.

Sitting legs folded on a faded rug, you and Atayib sip ghahawa together, a bowl of peanuts resting between you, as the words come in stop-start fashion. A five year absence. The language, of not knowing when or how to start, what to tell. You tell Atayib of your own marriage, your schooling, your hopes for a job. Your move from one monolithic city to the next. The streets of Chicago. The close rows of

Washington, D.C. That world seems so far it is as if you are lying. As if you are telling some tall tale of a land that lives only in the imagination.

It is then his turn. "I heard you saw my father," Atayib begins. "Did you notice his clouded eyes?" You reply that you did, that you had heard of his near-blindness.

"We journeyed all the way to N'Djamena. Stayed with family in the big city. It took us four hours just to find them after getting off the truck!" He proceeds to tell you of their journey—every day—across the pedestrian bridge to Cameroon. Where a single eye doctor practiced. Every day they would rise in the dark, say their prayers, drink their tea, before leaving for the bridge. At the bridge, they faced a fee that was up to the police and their whims. "500 francs one day. And the next day, 1,000!"

What little they had with them was stretched. Atayib's father could only afford treatment for one eye. So he chose his right, and the clouds cleared.

"It was a life that was not for us." They left on the next market truck back home to Ati.

You expect the story to end there. But Atayib stares out through the sunlit calico curtain, his lips still parted as if ready for more words. And then they come. "When our bus stopped along the road, and the passengers alighted to pray and eat, I received a phone call. They told me that my son had returned, that my sakhir had died."

The silence that follows hangs heavier than the cookfire soot at the end of day, the smoke mixed with the road dust kicked up by returning cows. So heavy it is hard to breathe. You had gone on to receive a degree, thinking your struggles to write, to live those first married years in one room apartments with college debt hovering over you, was any kind of struggle. Atayib, at the same time, had lost a child. As you sit next to your friend, you cannot fathom, cannot come close to say anything beyond the customary "kalawah." But the word seems incomplete, ill-fitting for a friend who has experienced the ultimate loss.

Atayib responds with a mumbled, "Allah yarhama." And then his face brightens, he springs to his feet and walks over to his bed, pulling out a small photo album from underneath the mattress.

When he opens the album, there is a picture you had given him—the photo of your youth basketball team, standing out on the crumbling cement court, each player squinting at the camera, yellow cotton jerseys bought from the market, stamped with the letters *J O R D A N*. There is Atayib. And there are others, too: Al Goni, Abdelmadjid, Bichara.

Atayib laughs. "Kay! Oh but we were quite the team back then, weren't we?" Together, you talk of the missed shots, the practices, the only play you knew to run, the pick and roll, and you talk about the long walks, throat parched, across town toward home, where you'd drink deep from the clay douane lying shaded at the base of the hajlij tree.

When the day's light begins to fade and you know the maghrib prayer will sound soon, you bid good-bye to your friend, and he walks you out to the door.

You know Atayib still farms. Still walks the eight kilometers out of town past the airport strip and the tattered windsock. Past the villages of MaTabke and Ammalaye. He walks all the way to the rows he tills with a rusted hoe. His hands sure of themselves, as the ground is upheaved, the seeds planted. And then the wait—and prayer—for the rain clouds rolling in from the south, reaching as far as they dare up toward the Saharan dunes. When the clouds finally split open, and the weighty drops pound the earth like falling shells, you imagine the shadow that must linger in the back of Atayib's mind. How it will be dampened, pushed back just for a little time. That green shoots will spring up from the earth around him. And when the next rainy season comes, he will begin the process all over again.

When your father agrees to visit the prison, the box-like fortress at the top of the town's few gentle hills, you ride along with him, your brother, and another of his doctor coworkers. An ancient colonial structure, you park outside and are led to a giant wood paneled door, with a much smaller human-sized door leading in. This is the first time, after all those years of growing up, that you see the inside of the place. The place where neighbors used to send family members to sober up. The place into which people would disappear then reappear after weeks, months. The place where, before it was renovated, had large gaping holes that inmates could walk straight out of to pick up wood for their small grill fires, or make tea and spread a mat out on the grounds and drink with the guards and play basara or arbatashar.

You find it much more crowded than you thought, the courtyard hardly living-room-sized, a bench set up for the medical professionals and a line of sick waiting to be treated. And you and your brother wander around, checking out the different barred wings, a guard letting you enter one, where a small well and some grass grows in the sunlight. You greet the prisoners resting in the shade, and then you hear one say your brother's name, *Bentley*. A voice parched from the heat of the day. When several of the men stand up, revealing the young man who had spoken from the ground, your brother recognizes an old soccer teammate, the one they called Loko, who spent his afternoons kicking up dust on the field and his nights playing tabla in the band of neighborhood sensation Abdoulaye Djime.

When later you drive away from this place, the medicine trunks empty of pills and your father exhausted, your brother looks out the window and shakes his head. "That was Loko. That was Loko." And you watch the colonial arches and the giant gutters and the paneled gate grow smaller in the side mirror, until it is a notch of whitewashed wall at the edge of a long dirtpacked road.

You walk back from watching a World Cup match at the neighborhood cinema—the yard packed so tightly with breathing bodies, heartbeats that throb together underneath the projected images of Luis Suarez at full sprint. You were noticed then—a boy calls your name in the dark. *Haroun, is that you?* But he is too young to know you, though when you were his age there was a friend who had his same shape, same eyes that pearl in the dark.

You walk back into the pure black of the streets beyond Chari Kabir, away from the city power lines. Only at the distance of a hundred yards do you see single bulbs here and there, illuminating the new walled houses built by Libyan families fleeing the violence of their home country hundreds of miles to the north. A whole Sahara away.

The town mud brick walls stretch out into the dark, becoming fewer, the open spaces becoming larger between them, framing a great expanse of earth, broken-up brick, and cowpies dotting the moon-reflective sand in the night.

It is in this open space, stars pinpricking the black above, when you see the staccato of flashlight. The dots, shining for half a second, disappear and reappear closer, then next show up beyond you, then shine no longer. Brief flashes to conserve battery.

But one light stops you. An old man and his son. The flashes had only told you there were two of differing height, and one was carrying a large, protective asa, blackened by soot and carved for walks such as this at night, when you don't know if you will face your neighbors for a chat along the road, or bandits. You can see in the circle glow of flashlight the lines of the father's face, tired from a day of heat and herding. And a boy whose eyes dilate from the darkness.

"Could you help us?" the man asks, taking in his breaths with the sand-wind, breathing in like the leaves of the nabakh trees around you. "We are looking for a sheep," he says. "Have you seen it?"

Your brother responds that he hasn't but that he'll keep his eye out for it.

You try to think if there's any animal you'd seen. There was the one sound of breathing and inhuman feet, but you could tell in the dark that it was a mutt trailing you before finding you uninteresting, finally melting away. You've always wondered about the city dogs, like half-sized buzz-cut wolves, howling in the distance. What would it take for the dogs to come upon you and your brother, two ghosts under the half-moon with meat still on bone? Perhaps it was because of this your brother had stopped a few minutes earlier to bend down and pick up a fist-sized rock. "For protection."

The old man wishes you a good night, but you wonder how long it will be before he turns home himself. He waves the beam of light across the field you are standing in, a group of plots waiting for new houses to be built on top—piles of bricks, trenches waiting for a foundation to be poured, tracks where horsecarts rumble down in daylight, loaded with building sand and straw. And around and between all this, parched desert shrubs spring up through construction rubble.

You make your way home, your eyes now meant to search for something. You think you see the sheep several times—but always only a trash bag tangled in a thorn bush or a pile of gray bricks broken in a slumbering pile. Always you ask your brother to place the beam on what you think will reveal the lost being; always you are disappointed.

You wonder about that old man in the night. Maybe he never turned back. Maybe he is always searching, through the night and heat of day, his son growing taller, the battery light flickering then going off one final time. Undeterred, he strides forward as his fathers did across the desert long ago. Lit by only the moon and najum.

You are on a ferry crossing the Bosphorus, the sun extinguishing itself in the west behind minarets and business towers, and from all around you, the call to prayer echoes from a hundred mosques—the rising and falling voice reverberates from Asia to Europe and back as you cross over to the western side of Istanbul.

You had wanted to cross over, to touch Asia, to wander around Üsküdar and see a different part of the city than what you were used to. You were hungry and so when you found a kebab shop, the spits rotating in the day's dying heat, you got yourself a sandwich and sat up on the second floor, a World Cup game on the television. You realized then, watching young couples come in and leave their dinner unattended between them, that you were in a part of the city that cared about Ramadan, and when you sit back, sandwich just finished, the owner comes to you and pleads with you in Turkish. "Sorry, I don't speak, Türkçe," you respond as you watch another restaurant worker turn off the television and you realize you are getting kicked out to make room for other customers coming in to break fast and you realize this is a mistake you would have chided yourself for when you were younger, flaunting food in the faces of those fasting.

"Epp sawak," a Chadian friend would have said as your cheeks burned, your eyes looking down.

You walk quickly out onto the street, trying to nod to the owner that you understand, that you realize your mistake. You wait in the park for the next ferry back as commuters rush from the dock to the taxis waiting for them, and families, just done with their prayers, wait in line beside a food truck. And when you are back on the ferry, back crossing the Bosphorus, you think not of the continent you have just left, but of the country, your country, that you had flown away from just a day before—leaving your friends behind again without knowing when you will return.

You wonder, as you watch the city rise before you, lights coming on, that perhaps you can remain here on this ferry—between who you were and who you have become. You wonder how you will return to the office desk again and sit down to your grad school classes—your other peers having gone on beach vacations or climbed mountains, but you, you have journeyed back through memory. You have sliced open the wounds of loss again and healed other bleeds. You have found that in the tea leaf silence more words can be expressed than in conversation. You have found that though years pass, you can still be the boy again who laughed with the ball in his hands or at his feet, who watched the cows come in at the close of day with wonder. You can still be the boy who walked with Al Goni and Bichara under the star-spread night, goat shadows passing around you, a night that seems like it will never fade.

You stand at the edge of Taksim Square with your brother, imagine a sea of protestors swarming through, protesting the rule of a president sucking out their right to speech everyday at a slow death-drip. The night silence floors you—that a place can be so alive in the light, then so dead, so slumbering, when the bulbs come on. Even then, the laughter and chatter of Istiklal Caddessi comes at you from behind, the mouth to the street full of neon street vendor lights and mannequin displays, where couples merge from side street cafes, buzzed or caffeinated, and walk with faces uplifted at the swirl of existence blazing before them. You feel the pull to return, to walk back the way you came, get ice cream from the shouting ice cream vendors, their thick arms beating the steel vats before scooping round orbs onto cones for passersby.

But your brother wants to see what another street will bring, a quiet street with a few scattered bars, parked motorcycles, and amber bulbs burning. He is always like this—always wanting to go back a different way—to *never see the same thing twice*—but you are so much more interested in going back, back down the rabbit hole to study the things you missed, to not let out of your sight what you had before. You exchange words, frustrations, and when he moves toward you, you shove him out of the way, your breathing labored, angered adrenaline cooling over your shoulders like holy water. In the space of a second, you see the fear in his eyes, imagine the fear in your own, hear his words, "What is wrong with you?" before you part, go your separate ways, needing a break.

As you walk the hour back to your hotel, back down the caddessi with the smiles and the wonder, its power is lost on you—you search in the faces for your brother, hoping just this once, he has come for you, you have come for him, and you will meet and say the real thing and not the stand-in thing. *We want to go back,* you imagine saying. *We want to go back to the date tree shade and the afternoon street wandering.* Back when you knew every sand street and the hour and second your friends would come and the ball would be in your hands and the laughter would ring out as measured and punctual as the muezzin's call.

Now, you have no language. Now, you have no words for what you see around you, what you feel within. A longing for your brother, a longing for the past, and a foreign city you've visited a handful of times, a city you love but can never attempt to understand.

You search for words you hope will describe your state. Words you hope will diagnose, treat, maybe even cure. You search and do not find them. Only when least looking does the language come from the corners of the globe—writers who have navigated the same life as you, the same in-between being.

You come across the words of Karin Desai, who in an interview asks the question, "What does it mean to return or to journey between worlds?" A question you cannot even attempt to answer. What does it really mean? Perhaps it is the journey that is the only part that makes sense—the journey in which you feel more at home in airport terminals, holding cardboard espresso cups in hand as you watch fellow travelers navigate from flight to flight, continent to continent.

You feel the worldweight of your own experience: a white boy who grew up a hundred miles south of Saharan dunes to American humanitarian aid worker parents. A white boy whose passport says "American" though you'd sooner feel at home on a grassmat underneath a nabakh tree, your friend Hissein or Al Goni or Atayib pouring tea. As boys, you did what normal kids do—kicked up dust with soccer balls, wandered around rivers skipping stones—your Arabic made chic with a peppering of street French. Your neighborhood was serenaded with the bellowing of camels, the lowing of cows as they marched home at sunset, down their own streets, each to their own home, walking unattended, guided only by the knowledge that their owner has set aside bowls of water and feed for them.

Other words come across your radar when you least expect them—the German *heimweh,* reductively meaning "homesickness," a word that fits nearer the mark but it is the "home" part of that word you struggle to perceive. Or Orhan Pamuk's *huzun*, the Turkish eternal melancholy, used to define the sense that Istanbullus feel when living in the shadow of their great national past. Living in the shadow, yes, but for you the borders are so much more fluid, the nation that beckons you impossible to pinpoint on a map.

And then you come across the Welsh word *hiraeth*, a grief-tinged longing for home—but not a home one can return to. Rather, a wistful longing for the place of one's past, knowing that the past can never be restored. The past can only live on in the clutches of memory. Cradled in the mind just as it morphs and shape-shifts, memory becoming something else entirely.

The language seems to fail the fullness of your experience. A melancholy, a longing, a sickness. Where is the cure? Only in a friend's words, the kaleidoscopic flash of a smile, given to you when the mind slows, opening itself up to the past just as much as the past reaches into present.

You are on a bus in Maryland, bussing down Annapolis Road on your way back to your job at the university. You stare at the men and women around you—the college students going to summer school, the old woman in a polo and white tennis shoes off to work, and the retired football coach heading to the stadium to watch a practice. You wonder if they can taste sand salt on you, see the desert on your fresh-washed clothes, if they can smell the dry fields and the first scent of rainy season wind.

Later, when you are back home in your apartment, Ethiopian music pulsing through the walls, you try to type out the beginnings of a poem and then another. On the bus the next day, you write more lines—"trying to find the music again," you write; "always, I walk through the sandshadow, bursting its chest," you write; "waiting in suburbia for the myth of life to return," you write. You realize you are writing the same poem over and over, the same line, the same sentence, trying to get back to what you had just seen, what you had just felt again during your five-year return to the place of your past, the place of who you were, who you are.

You tried to force your way back. Tried to figure out a way to return to the mythic life, the life of memory and Arabic. You applied for a teaching job in Oman, stayed up late for a 2 a.m. Skype interview in which two men in kaffia turbans asked you how you would get your students to describe a nearby mountain during a class session—the kind of interview question that leaps up on you from behind. *I would tell them to write a letter, to write a letter to someone who is not there, who cannot see the mountain for themselves. I would tell them to describe the mountain, to describe a journey up it.*

You got the job, and with your wife, you packed up your apartment in Maryland, the walls covered in stacked boxes—your journey across oceans once again approaching. You had wrestled with the choice—why were you doing this? You tortured yourself as if you were chasing some experience, some thrill, some maneuver to force your way back into the old life again. When you finally convinced yourself of the rightness of your decision, signed the contract, structured your life around the oncoming change—you received an email, subject line reading, *visa application denied.* The university contact wishing you *better luck next year!*

You lay down in your packed-up apartment and knew then that the way back to the past is barred, try as you might to recreate it; that the wrong motivations—trying to use them rightly—had sealed up every road you've tried to construct, every path through and around the lived experience of now. You imagined yourself returning from a day's worth of teaching, your skin encrusted with dust and sweat, and in the twilight night, you thought you'd have a child to guide around a dirt yard in the shade of a twisted tree. You thought you'd ride in trucks with friends all the way up the mountain—or into the dunes—and pause for moments looking out on the drybone curves. You pictured yourself sipping mint tea by the ocean waves instead of driving a four-lane highway through Maryland suburbia, the dissonance vibrating between office buildings, crab shacks, car dealerships.

You tried, almost begged, for a chance back through the visa process—but knew you were fighting fate in your deepest being. You found another job, a teaching job not in the Middle East but in the Midwest. Here, the days end in dust just like they did. Here, at night you can walk out and watch the Milky Way just as you did. Here, a train of camels walks the acres around an exotic animal farm, and you remember the camels your neighbor would string up to the sewage tree or the camels loping through town on market day. And here, everyone knows what everyone does, just like they did before. But you are not the American here, not the foreigner grafted in, embraced yet always held apart. Here, you are Chadian, the one who walked the world and back, the one whose skin looks like everyone else, but one who carries an immaterial weight of difference. You are held even farther apart than you were elsewhere. The one who dreamed in Arabic and wandered airports as if they were the halls of home. The one who looks up at the sky and feels the distance between earth and air, the blazing wind that picks up sand and sweeps it across the road like a gentle caress.

It is your birthday—sixteen or seventeen—and you have taken over the living room with your friends. There is Bichara with his brother, Al Goni, telling a story about a boy in school who got in a fight that day. How the boy swore to duel another student, and how they marched off outside of town to face each other—but then they turned and ran away, both too scared to fight.

There is Atayib leaning back and laughing at the story. Others—Abdelmadjid, Hassan, Hissein, Djiddo. Food is brought in by the sufra-full, plates of pizza and hamburgers, the American akil your friends requested. The group goes silent as you gather around, a chorus of *bismillah* coming from those around you as you all then dig in with your fingers—lips smacking, Abdelmadjid talking about how he could eat this all day. You make short work of the meal, the plates emptied, the tray littered with the remains of the dinner as if a battleground. Atayib leans back and burps.

And then someone—Hassan—rises and says, "Yallah, it is time to sing 'Happy Birthday.'" And then as one your friends stand to their feet, a few holding the confetti poppers you had brought from America above their heads and you are all laughing as your friends stumble through the song they've managed to pick up in English over the years: "Happy birrday, to-to! Happy birrday, two-three!" and then the confetti is shot out over your heads as your friends whoop and crumple to the floor in gut-splitting laughter. Plastic swirls of purple and green and gold landing all around them.

***

You wish it could all be given to you again—this richness, this old life where you were as one though the war storms threatened, succeeded even, to separate you. You would do it all over again—yes, the rush of adrenaline as the bullets thudded, the slow dull pain in the heart not knowing whether you will stay one day or flee the next because of rebel offensives. You would do it all over again if for a minute of time when you were together as brothers, the metal grinder in the corner whirring as Al Goni makes mango smoothies, the basketball bouncing outside as Atayib tries to hone his shot. You would do it all again to be together once more with Madri, to see the flash of his smile, hear his half-laughed jokes. To not know that he will soon lie buried somewhere in the dry earth with a brick as his headstone. No one really knowing which brick marks the place. Which earth patch marks a grave of a friend too soon gone.

You are left now to meet only in your memories.

acknowledgments

Excerpts from this book have been published in *Waxwing*, *Whale Road Review*, and *Windhover*, and have been nominated for the *2019 Best of the Net* anthology.

about the author

Born in Texas and raised in Chad, Aaron Brown is the author of the poetry collection, *Acacia Road*, winner of the 2016 Gerald Cable Book Award (Silverfish Review Press). He has been published in *World Literature Today, Tupelo Quarterly, Waxwing, Cimarron Review*, and *Transition*, among others, and he is a contributing editor for *Windhover*. Brown now lives in Texas, where he is an assistant professor of English and directs the writing center at LeTourneau University. He holds an MFA from the University of Maryland.

about the press

Unsolicited Press is based out of Portland, Oregon and focuses on the works of the unsung and underrepresented. As a womxn-owned, all-volunteer small publisher that doesn't worry about profits as much as championing exceptional literature, we have the privilege of partnering with authors skirting the fringes of the lit world. We've worked with emerging and award-winning authors such as Shann Ray, Amy Shimshon-Santo, Brook Bhagat, Kris Amos, and John W. Bateman.

Learn more at Unsolicitedpress.com. Find us on Twitter, Instagram, Facebook, Pinterest, Threads, TikTok, and YouTube at @UnsolicitedP.

www.ingramcontent.com/pod-product-compliance
Lightning Source LLC
Chambersburg PA
CBHW021447070526
44577CB00002B/295